Praise For
Mindfulness Meets Emotional Awareness

"What a wealth of insights Jenny's book provides on the impact of emotions, on our lives and choices.

For years I have been advocating the positive significance of questions that generate greater self-awareness and self-responsibility. You can't determine what life throws at you, your choice is how you react. Awareness is the key to making wiser decisions.

Jenny provides illustration and insights which help provide new ways of seeing and handling emotional challenges. She has broken down the huge area into themes and within these provided useful guidelines and understanding. It is only when delving deeply and with honesty, into our own way of being that we can gain the value of choosing to modify our perspectives and/or behaviour.

Emotion can be read as e-motion - energy in motion. Jenny asks us to notice the difference in our energy with positive or negative focus on ourselves.

She asks us to listen to our heart and our gut. How well do we truly listen to ourselves, as well as others? It is a book well worth our engagement – a truly helpful addition to awareness."

Dr David Hemery

CBE DL, Olympic hurdling champion, coach, teacher, author and founder of the Charity for schools, 21st Century Legacy and the 'Be the Best you can Be!' program.

www.21stcenturylegacy.com

"Thoughtful, Articulate and Essential…

This book will teach you how to establish a healthy communication between your reason and your emotions"

Alicia Heraz,
Eng. PhD. Founder and CEO Emotions Matter

"A step by step, low technology, high impact, guide to emotional awareness.

This lovely book takes the reader on a profound journey. It is a significant resource that really creates genuine opportunity for self-development and growth.

The steps are clear and the processes simple.

I read it as a resource for others but then found the content and language so engaging and relevant that it prompted a personal review of my own responses.

Thank you, Jenny."

Libby Alderson Chartered Fellow FCIPD
Organizational Coach and Supervisor. Learning Excellence Manager

"This valuable book reminds us of the importance of our emotions.

The daily invitations provide practical exercises that enable us to learn to pause and reflect, to be able to notice what our feelings are trying to tell us.

Beautifully written and easy to navigate."

Dr Laura Hill
Counselling Psychologist. BPS Chartered HCPC Accredited

"A thoroughly enjoyable read, Jenny has communicated to her audience in such a direct and concise way, exploring the essence of the struggles we all face with these most difficult and common "negative" emotions.

The book has thrown light on specific emotions, such as anger, fear, anxiety, sadness, envy and shame and challenges us to engage differently, using positive thinking and acceptance of our difficult feelings.

A book which is accessible to everyone, easy to read and can be referred back to time and again."

Jo Turner
PG Dip. Mar. Th. Psychodynamic Relationship
Psychotherapist

"This easily accessible book provides insight into how our relationship with our feelings affects our both our peace of mind and our capability in the world.

It also provides an excellent tool kit to address our issues with "difficult" feelings and learn how to embrace and accept them in service of developing a more calm, purposeful and richer life."

Heather Garbutt M.A.
Relationship Coach and Psychotherapist
Director of The Counselling & Psychotherapy Centre,
Swindon, U.K.

A Message from the Author

I wrote this book to create 'Real' change within our everyday 'Real' human lives!

Mental Health problems such as anxiety and depression are on the increase and we are seeing epidemics of the kinds of problems whose origins stem from an inability to navigate relationships from a position of health and vitality. Loneliness is considered the third-largest problem in the United States and The World Health Organization has labelled depression as the single leading cause of disability globally. Greater than either heart disease or cancer. People are not happy!

It has been my experience both professionally and personally that many of humanities problems have their roots in an inability to manage emotions. Emotionally reactive behavior is a constant source of conflict, not only within our closest relationships, but also in the world at large.

If our external world is indeed simply a mirror of our internal world, then the conflict that we see on a global scale must surely highlight, that internally we have some significant work to do. If we are to create any degree of peace in the world at large, we are going to have to discover some way to find peace within ourselves. If we are going to generate equality in the world, we will need to recognize those deep-seated legacies of the past that hibernate within us all, surfacing sometimes in direct and obvious ways and yet at other times manifest unconsciously, subtly coloring our responses and our actions in ways that may inadvertently replicate and generate more of the same.

I wrote this book to create 'Real' change within our 'Real' everyday human lives!

Within these pages, readers will discover a new appreciation and understanding of our most challenging emotions, not as something that we need to fear and do battle with, but as vital components in our ability to successfully navigate the peaks and troughs of a normal human life, particularly within the realm of our relationships.

If we are to overcome our differences and learn to appreciate and truly value the diversity that we each as individuals bring to the collective whole of humanity we will need to understand ourselves, not only through the power and empowerment of our mind, but through an empowerment forged in connection of our emotions, that vital human component that enables us to be 'alive feeling', compassionate human beings. And in doing so we create the potential for harmonious resolution of problems, not only in the immediacy of our own lives but for the well-being of humanity at large.

Thank you.

Mindfulness Meets Emotional Awareness

More Books from the Author

This is the second book in Jenny's series about the Intelligence of our Emotions

7 Steps to Spiritual Empathy, the first book in the series is available from Amazon in Kindle, Paperback and in Audio.

This book is overflowing with kindness, insight, depth and above all...love."
Katherine Woodward Thomas,
New York Times Bestselling Author of Calling in "The One"

7 STEPS TO SPIRITUAL EMPATHY

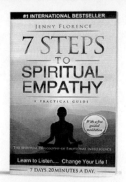

Self-Care is NOT an Act of Selfishness,
it is an Act of Consciousness.

Learning to Listen to Our Emotions
is a Primary Act of Care,
Enabling Care of Ourselves, Care of
Others, and Care of the World at Large.

Empathy is so much more than just a Cognitive Listening Skill!

https://amzn.to/2GaqgoN Amazon.com USA
https://amzn.to/2DTbxfK Amazon.co.uk UK
https://amzn.to/2RFsTjU Amazon Audible

Mindfulness Meets Emotional Awareness

Launching in early 2019

I Choose Love, the Pathway of the Spiritual Warrior, an A-Z Guide. Available from Amazon in Kindle, Paperback and in Audio.

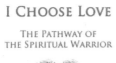

For further information please visit Jenny's Amazon Author Pages.

https://amzn.to/2UH4tIO USA
https://amzn.to/2DRtJXo UK

To access further resources that support all aspects of Emotional Health, join Jenny's FREE online Library.

www.azemotionalhealth.com

www.azemotionalhealth.com

Membership to the Library is completely FREE and always will be.

Mindfulness Meets Emotional Awareness

Mindfulness Meets Emotional Awareness

7 Steps to Learn the Language of your Emotions

Change your Perspective... Change your Life!

The second in the series of books

"The Intelligence of Our Emotions"

By
Jenny Florence

Mindfulness Meets Emotional Awareness
The Empowerment of Emotional Literacy

First Published 2017 A-Z of Emotional Health
Copyright © Jenny Florence/Jenny Burgess 2016

ISBN 978-0-9955079-2-0

About this Book.

This book is pragmatic, down-to-earth and free of psychological jargon.

In just seven days, readers are guided on a step-by-step comprehensive journey that introduces each of our most challenging emotions with clear understanding as to why every single emotion that we have is necessary, valuable and serves a purpose.

Bite-sized chapters can be read in just 20-25 minutes a day and can be returned to easily during any emotionally challenging times.

Daily Invitations

Each chapter contains an additional section of pragmatic invitations and exercises that are designed to integrate and expand emotional knowledge and awareness into everyday real-life situations.

Self-awareness is often likened to the layers of an onion. Each time we apply a chapter to a particular situation, either for the first time or in returning again, the daily invitations are designed to enable another layer of emotional awareness to unfold.

As we expand our awareness, we can in turn discover how to actively use our emotions as a vital ally in navigating our lives successfully.

Additional Free Resources

Emotional Meditation

A 15 Day Series of Meditations based on this book can be accessed through Jenny's on-line Library. The A-Z of Emotional Health. A free public resource dedicated to raising the awareness of Emotional Health and the empowerment of Emotional Literacy.

www.azemotionalhealth.com

If you would like to receive updates about Jenny's work, please register your details on her homepage.

www.jennyflorencehealth.com

Dedication

*"Your ordinary acts of love and hope point to the extraordinary promise that every human life is of inestimable value.
Do your little bit of good where you are; it's those little bits of good put together that overwhelm the world."*

Desmond Tutu. (b.1931) Leader

I wish to dedicate this book to all of you who are striving to make a positive difference in this world.

I am sure that on a daily basis, we all come across situations, people and circumstances that generate within us negative and challenging emotions. When we look around us locally, nationally and globally we will find ourselves witness to acts of human destruction and difficulty that step over the bounds of what must surely constitute the qualities of what it is to be a decent and caring human being.

However, in noticing a problem, we are actually being presented with an opportunity.

We define ourselves not only through our good experiences... but also through those experiences that challenge us and push us to our limits.

It is my experience that the greatest changes... that make the greatest difference, take place within the 'ordinariness' of our everyday, real lives.

Mindfulness Meets Emotional Awareness

When faced with a problem, a difficulty or a challenge, what we each choose to do in response, our attitudes toward the situation and our subsequent actions, can make the difference between a problem being compounded and repeated, or alternatively, worked through, resolved and laid to rest.

And in this we have a choice.

Consciously embracing an attitude of self-responsibility, kindness, compassion, care and above all respect... sends a ripple out into the world that creates far more positive change than we as individuals can ever be fully aware of.

Thank you to all of you, who in the extraordinary ordinary ways, that are so often unrecognized and yet make such a difference, choose to live as you do. In doing so, you shine.

In choosing to live respectfully we embrace our unique individual ability to be the cutting edge of change.

It is within the immediacy of our own lives that we sow the seeds of real and significant change and in being the best that we can be and in supporting others to do the same, we create a beacon of hope for others to follow.

"It's always inspiring to me to meet people who feel that they can make a difference in the world. That's their motive, that's their passion... I think that's what makes your life meaningful, that's what fills your own heart and that's what gives you purpose."

Maria Shriver. (b.1955) Journalist

Mindfulness Meets Emotional Awareness

Contents

Introduction   **17**
The Collaboration of Mindfulness and Emotional Awareness

How to Use this Book   **25**
The Empowerment of Emotional Literacy
My invitation for today   **31**

Chapter 1   **39**
Healthy Fear and Healthy Anxiety
My invitation for today   **54**

Chapter 2   **61**
Healthy Shame and Guilt
My invitation for today   **73**

Chapter 3   **81**
Healthy Anger and Aggression
My invitation for today   **92**

Chapter 4   **99**
Healthy Disappointment
My invitation for today   **112**

Chapter 5   **117**
Despair; The Ultimate Wake Up Call!
My invitation for today   **126**

Chapter 6   **137**
Healthy Sadness
My invitation for today   **148**

Chapter 7   155
Healthy Envy and Jealousy
My invitation for today   169

Conclusion   175
Taking Responsibility and an "Ownership" of our Emotions

Review Request   185

About the Author and this Series of Books   187

Work with Jenny   191

References   192

Mindfulness Meets Emotional Awareness

Introduction

The Collaboration of Mindfulness and Emotional Awareness

"In the last decade or so, science has discovered a tremendous amount about the role that emotions play in our lives. Researchers have found that even more than IQ, your emotional awareness and abilities to handle feelings will determine your success and happiness in all walks of life, including family relationships."

John Gottman (b. 1942), Professor Emeritus in Psychology

Few of us, if any at all, will experience a lifetime of ongoing contentment and blissful harmony, without any ups and downs or life challenges. Indeed, we wouldn't be human if we did.

In truth, it is frequently our greatest challenges in life that ultimately bring us our greatest moments of growth and learning. It is often adversity that propels us to greater levels of awareness and solidifies the formation of our core inner values, supporting a true appreciation of who we are and of what we have and who we may wish to be.

So what makes this possible? What makes it possible to manage the tough times and come out on the other side not only "intact" but feeling stronger because of it?

In my experience, both professionally in listening to literally hundreds of people within my therapeutic practice, spanning 26 years, as well as personally within my own life circumstances, central to this possibility is the relationship between our mind and our emotions.

There is a direct relationship between the way that we think and the way that we feel. Our mind and our emotions affect and influence one another.

If our thoughts are negative and bleak it will affect the way that we feel; negative thoughts will generate negative and challenging emotions. Likewise, if we are feeling unhappy or low this will colour our thoughts and our perceptions and we will be far more likely to perceive situations and indeed other people with negative expectations.

However logical we may think that we are, our emotions are always in play, unseen and often unacknowledged.

We have a continual emotional interaction with whatever's going on around us, as well as an emotional response to this and one of the greatest challenges that we face at times of difficulty is how to manage the intense emotions that arise.

Even on an everyday basis, our emotions can sometimes prove to be confusing and hard to understand. If our mind hasn't learned to identify and to understand our emotions, then any kind of intense emotionally-laden experience will present us with a potential difficulty. We won't know how to interpret the way that we are feeling, and how to handle ourselves in that moment.

Anyone who has ever struggled with intense and overwhelming emotions at times of stress, duress or challenge will know how extraordinarily difficult it is to remain grounded in these moments, and what a challenge it is to remain confident, not only in our interactions with others but also in our belief in ourselves and in our feelings of self-worth, self-value and self-esteem.

Healthy self-esteem and a core sense of inner personal well-being doesn't come from blocking out our more uncomfortable feelings. It comes from listening to our feelings and attending to them responsively; this enables us to be resilient and 'to be okay' regardless of what's going on in our world. For this to take place, our mind will need to be aware of and receptive to our emotions.

When we talk about being mindful and we teach mindfulness, our desire is to enable people to develop the skill of becoming more 'present'. In calming the 'internal noise' of the mind we can become more reflective and more aware of what is going on, both in and around us within the immediacy of our environment.

When we develop our awareness of the present moment, we are actually developing our ability to be fully relational.

We are living beings, in constant interaction with the world around us. Even in sleep, we are still connected or 'in relationship' with the world around us. A sudden noise might wake us up.

Mindfulness Meets Emotional Awareness

When we develop our ability to be fully present, we are learning to listen and to hear; not simply with our ears, but to relate with our actual experience in the immediacy of the present moment.

We are learning to listen to life as a fully relational person and this will involve not only calming our thoughts to enable us to have a clarity of perception within the moment, but it will also involve an awareness of our emotional experience. It will involve being aware of and listening to our emotions.

Human beings are first and foremost relational creatures. Our primary drive is to connect and to relate with others and this is not simply a question of thought. Our relationships and our ability to relate with others is rooted in our emotional experience, our relationships with others are rooted in the emotional bonds that we build, and yet the majority of us will not have grown up in a world that acknowledges the power of our emotions let alone taught us the necessary skills and the emotional intelligence to navigate our lives with an awareness of both thought and feeling and the powerful interaction between them.

Our thoughts and perceptions are influenced and colored by our emotions and likewise our emotions are equally affected by the way that we think. An underlying state of emotional unease fuels negative thinking patterns and perceptions. In turn, a negative state of mind will generate emotions that mirror this unease.

Left unattended this interaction can create a downward spiral in both mind and feeling. When we ignore our emotions, we do so at our peril.

Mindfulness Meets Emotional Awareness

There is a strong link between our ability to 'read' ourselves emotionally and our capacity for self-care. If we lack an awareness or a 'connection' to our emotional responses we are missing vital information that serves a primary function in our ability to look after ourselves. We need this emotional information to assist and inform our choices and our decisions.

How many times have all of us NOT listened to the way that we were feeling, and pushed through regardless, only to later regret doing so? I know there have been countless occasions when I have done this myself.

Sometimes my actions followed what I believed that I *should* be doing, rather than what actually would have *felt* right. Sometimes I simply didn't want to listen to my feelings because the outcome would mean acknowledging something that I didn't really want to hear. It wasn't what I really wanted so I continued on my fixed course, overriding what later proved to be extremely 'good information'. In each of these scenarios, my mind was overriding my natural ability to navigate my life from a position of well-informed, responsive, self-care.

I think it is useful here to define a difference here between an 'inner' or a 'gut' feeling, something deep within us that holds an inner knowing or an inner wisdom, which some people refer to as our 'higher self,' as opposed to emotional feelings, and yet both play a part in our ability to navigate our lives successfully.

Mindfulness Meets Emotional Awareness

Like an internal satnav system our emotional feeling is giving us a constant flow of information, and curiously enough, when we do not listen to our 'inner' or 'gut' feeling, it is our emotions that surface in response to this that will let us know in no uncertain terms that we have navigated 'off-course'.

Given that this book is written to deepen our emotional awareness, when I refer to 'feelings' unless otherwise stated I am referring to feelings of an emotional nature.

Our self-awareness and the resulting state of self-responsibility is an ongoing, ever evolving state of being and an inability to listen to ourselves can come about for many reasons.

Sometimes we don't listen to ourselves not because we don't really want to, but because we simply don't know how to.

If we are a reasonably self-aware individual this may seem strange, but sometimes we can be far more open to listening to others than we are to ourselves and this can get in the way of our capacity for self-care.

Many of us carry unconscious messages that in our adult lives, actually stop us from acting in our own best interests, indeed sometimes our attempts at self-care can even inadvertently sabotage our ability to move our lives forwards.

In truth if we have never been given a clear and supportive role model to follow, then developing an attitude of healthy self-care will be a life skill that we will need to learn. Learning to listen to ourselves with an awareness of our emotions plays an integral role in living from a position of healthy self-care.

Mindfulness Meets Emotional Awareness

Our ability to listen primarily to ourselves is a core relational skill, a skill that is fueled by the collaborative meeting of our mind and our emotions, which in turn enables us to listen and to relate with others.

There is a relativity between our ability to 'read' others emotionally and our capacity to build and to sustain healthy relationships.

When our decisions and choices come from a position of true 'self-responsibility' they will demonstrate an awareness of our own needs, as well as an awareness of the consequences of our decisions and actions and therefore an awareness of the needs of others.

Wisdom is the outcome of knowledge and experience integrating together. A collaborative relationship between our mind and our emotions actively enables this process to take place.

Our mind and our emotions make a very powerful team. When they work well, this collaborative relationship will support us in navigating our lives responsively.

"Part of the problem with the word 'disabilities' is that it immediately suggests an inability to see or hear or walk or do other things that many of us take for granted.

But what of people who can't feel? Or talk about their feelings? Or manage their feelings in constructive ways? What of people who aren't able to form close and strong relationships?

Mindfulness Meets Emotional Awareness

And people who cannot find fulfilment in their lives, or those who have lost hope, who live in disappointment and bitterness and find in life no joy, no love?

These, it seems to me, are the real disabilities."

Fred Rogers (b. 1928), television personality

How to Use this Book
The Empowerment of Emotional Literacy

"Helping people better manage their upsetting feelings; anger, anxiety, depression, pessimism, and loneliness is a form of disease prevention.
Since the data shows that the toxicity of these emotions, when chronic, is on a par with smoking cigarettes, helping people handle them better could potentially have a medical payoff as great as getting heavy smokers to quit."

Daniel Goleman (b. 1946), author, psychologist, and science journalist

How to use this book and how to get the very best from it.

This book is designed to build and to develop, to extend and to enhance your emotional vocabulary and the fluency of your emotional language.

In my work as a therapist I continually meet people who are experiencing challenging times and the one common denominator that I find, regardless of individual circumstances, is that every single person that I meet is struggling to relate to the way that they are feeling.

They are struggling to understand their emotional experiences.

Even when their feelings are completely appropriate and a natural response to the kind of things that are taking place in their world at that time, they feel emotionally overwhelmed and they don't know how to handle this or how to cope.

They lack an understanding of the way that they feel and they have no emotional language and no emotional vocabulary that will enable them to relate, understand and engage with what's actually going on for them.

It is not uncommon for people to struggle to talk about their feelings and to make sense of them. This can come about for many reasons.

Sometimes we are fearful of what others may think of us. Many of us grew up in a world where showing any kind of emotion, beyond our happy feelings, was frowned upon or discouraged and as a consequence we may have developed all kinds of internal perceptions and inner messages within our mind that leave us feeling bad... about feeling bad!

Sometimes we simply have no idea why we are feeling the way that we do. Our emotions seem random; we wake up not feeling ok without any understanding of *why*.

This can feel frightening and challenges us beyond belief, we feel as though we ourselves are out of our own control and can end up becoming fearful of our own feelings. Fearful of the power of our own emotions!

Mindfulness Meets Emotional Awareness

For others, while emotions may not necessarily have been labelled as negative or unacceptable, we may simply have grown up in an environment in which no one ever spoke about their feelings; so we have never had the opportunity to learn a language or an emotional vocabulary that would allow us to develop an understanding within ourselves that would enable us to process and to understand our emotional experiences.

If we grew up in a world where our parents didn't have an emotional language themselves, not because they were bad or inadequate parents, but because they themselves had grown up in a world where their parents had no emotional language either, then this incredibly helpful life skill will be missing. We won't be well equipped.

Having an emotional language and an emotional vocabulary is a valuable life skill: it establishes a connection between our emotional experience and our mind, a link between experience and thought.

Language is descriptive, our words and the vocabulary that we use helps us to define something and to make sense of it. In doing so we create the opportunity to gain a greater understanding and a greater comprehension of what something may mean.

Language sits at the heart of communication.

The health of any relationship will be reliant upon a good level of communication and this includes the kind of internal communication that we have within ourselves.

Mindfulness Meets Emotional Awareness

We all have an inner dialogue or conversation that takes place within our mind. If we are faced with intense emotions during a challenging life experience and the kinds of conversation that take place within our mind are encouraging, supportive, mindful and compassionate this will help us to find our way through any adversity.

However, if our internal dialogue is dismissive of our emotions or judgmental and full of criticism, this will erode our emotional durability, lower our confidence and undermine our self-esteem, potentially generating even more challenging emotions in what is already a stressful situation.

Our ability to listen primarily to ourselves is a core relational skill, a skill that is fueled by the collaborative meeting of our mind and our emotions. This in turn enables us to listen and to relate with others.

Being emotionally healthy isn't about being happy all of the time.

The basis of emotional health is about being able to understand and be responsive to our emotional experiences and to be able to feel the full range of our emotions and for our mind to remain at relative ease with this.

Even in adversity, it is through the meeting of our emotional experience combined with reflective thought that we make sense of our life experiences; in doing so we discover and we develop meaning in life.

Mindfulness Meets Emotional Awareness

Developing meaning in life is not just a mental process, it is not simply a question of thought. Our value systems and the things that matter to us are a direct result of the way that we *feel* about things. Our emotions let us know what matters to us.

When we talk about 'quality of life', what we are really talking about is the way that we feel.

When we talk about 'quality time', whether it is quality 'me time' or 'quality time' spent with someone else — whether we are in a fabulous restaurant, cuddled up on the sofa watching TV or sitting on top of a mountain watching the sunset — we are talking about the quality of the time that we are experiencing, the way that we feel and the meaning that these experiences bring to our lives.

Our capacity to develop meaning from an experience is a direct result of a connection and a relatedness between the awareness of our mind and our emotional state of being.

Sometimes this connection and relatedness is missing.

Our emotions are cut off, or experienced as separate and so are then disconnected from any form of mindfulness or considered thought.

When this happens, people can get into very deep water because they find themselves being very emotionally reactive. Unable to 'pause for thought', they react in the immediacy of the moment. In this instance, they are being driven entirely by their emotions. Reflective considered thought is absent.

Mindfulness Meets Emotional Awareness

Certain emotions will generate a huge amount of energy: in the absence of a connection between our mind and our emotions, our capacity for mindful considered thought is diminished.

This fuels a reactive state of living that is always highly emotionally charged.

When we can take considered actions that are reflective, thoughtful and based in conscious choice, rather than generating emotionally charged *re-actions*, life tends to run far more smoothly.

When our mind can listen to and receive our emotions, and with reflection, make considered, conscious choices, we become far more in charge of our actions and therefore far more in charge of our own lives.

The connection between our mind and emotions and the fluency of our 'internal emotional language' will enable us to make sense of the way that we feel in any given circumstance both good or challenging.

This connection will underpin our capacity to negotiate our daily life experiences, even the challenging ones, with confidence, durability and resilience.

My invitation for today

Today I wish to invite you to develop your capacity to be mindful of your emotions and to develop a structure that will enable you to extend, to enhance and to build your emotional language.

My thought for today

"Learn to listen without preconception or judgement."

The starting point of any form of increasing awareness is to begin to notice and where better to start than within ourselves?

If we are unable to comprehend our own emotional experiences, then we are unlikely to comprehend the feelings and emotions of others.

To really use our emotions as the bringers of good and valuable information, we will need to become adept at identifying and listening to them. This will include an ability to recognize our individual emotions.

Because our thoughts and feelings are so interlaced, we often don't notice the difference between them, let alone our own internal mental attitude towards our emotions.

Mindfulness Meets Emotional Awareness

If we lack understanding of our individual emotions — and as a consequence, become fearful of feeling a particular emotion — then in doing so we are inadvertently generating a secondary package of emotion on top of an already challenging experience.

If we 'feel bad - about feeling bad' then we have just doubled the emotional load!

If we become 'anxious - about feeling anxiety' then we have just doubled the emotional load!

If we become 'angry and frustrated - because we are feeling angry and frustrated' then we have just doubled the emotional load!

This is such a common experience, and is incredibly unhelpful for us. The last thing we need at times of emotional difficulty is to make ourselves feel even worse!

A very good starting point to tackle this kind of response is to extend our emotional language in a way that will help us to re-frame the way in which we perceive our emotions.

Emotions are frequently talked about in a very black and white kind of language. I often hear them described as either good or bad, positive or negative.

We feel good today or we feel bad today. We feel positive or we feel negative. Our mood is high or low. We're up or we're down.

Mindfulness Meets Emotional Awareness

To my mind this is far too limiting and restricting as it doesn't allow us to recognize our individual emotions at all and it certainly doesn't do justice to the range of emotions that we have, or indeed acknowledge the importance of all of them.

When our emotions are perceived within this limited scope of language it can significantly inhibit our ability to listen to what we are feeling and to look more deeply for the root cause of any kind of emotional distress or difficulty that we may be facing.

This very black and white terminology automatically tends to raise anxiety whenever we feel anything that we perceive as bad and so contributes to us turning up the intensity volume and effectively 'doubling the emotional load' in what was already a challenging situation.

So today I wish to gently challenge any internal perceptions that you may hold in your mind about your emotional states, and I would like to invite you to redefine and reclassify your feelings.

I will still use two categories with just two different headings, but rather than the black and white, good/bad, positive/negative version, my two headings are going to be classified as:

'The Easy, Comfortable Emotions' – versus - 'The Uneasy, Uncomfortable Emotions'

It's not difficult to identify either of these categories.

Mindfulness Meets Emotional Awareness

The easy comfortable camp is full of the happy, relaxed, joyous, pleasurable emotions; the uneasy uncomfortable camp is full of the more challenging, difficult feelings we have such as fear, guilt, anxiety, and anger.

None of these feelings and emotions are bad.

Every emotional state that we experience is actually informing us; whatever we are feeling, whether it's easy or uneasy, comfortable or uncomfortable, our emotions are telling us something important. It's an important piece of navigational information.

We need to learn to listen to this information so that it can support us in making informed and appropriate choices in our lives, particularly during times of stress and difficulty.

A Useful Exercise

Using a piece of paper or your journal take some time to pause. And as you pause bring your attention to yourself.

You may wish to bring a particular situation to mind. If this is the case, give your mind a few moments to focus on the scenario.

Letting go of any preconceptions, associations or judgements, both good or bad, that you may carry about specific emotions, notice what you are feeling in this present moment and become aware of any specific emotions that are present. Also notice any sensations in your physical body: are you relaxed, are you tense?

Mindfulness Meets Emotional Awareness

Draw a line down the middle of the page and on one side list everything that you are feeling. Try not to edit yourself. Give yourself the freedom to just listen and to write without any form of judgement or interpretation. Simply listen and become an observer of the way that you feel.

When you have finished, ask yourself these questions, making any notes and observations on the other side of the page.

- Were you fully aware of the way that you were feeling, or have your emotions only come to your attention because you have paused and taken conscious time to notice?
- How easily were you able to identify your different emotions? Is your mind familiar with the different emotional states that you feel? Many of us are not!
- Do you perceive any of these emotions in black and white terms, good or bad, positive or negative?
- Are you aware of any thinking patterns that may be contributing to the intensity of the emotions that you have noticed?
- Are you 'doubling the load'?
- Do any of your emotions generate further emotions?

Now using two new fresh pages, one for each of the two new categories of the 'easy and comfortable' and the 'uneasy and uncomfortable' feelings, I would invite you to re-list all of the emotions that you have identified.

Any that fall under the easy, more comfortable heading are a validation and should be listened to, acknowledged, appreciated and — if appropriate — celebrated!

Mindfulness Meets Emotional Awareness

Any that fall under the more challenging heading are requiring your attention.

In the latter case, without any form of judgement or criticism, take some time to consider what it is that these feelings may be trying to tell you. How do they relate to the situation that you brought to mind?

Our more challenging emotions are very often a 'call to action'. Something needs to change.

If you are uncertain about any of your feeling states, then the most appropriate 'call to action' in this moment may be to firstly gain a greater understanding of this emotion, whilst giving yourself permission to take time for reflection before engaging in any kind of decision-making.

If any of these feelings are so extreme in intensity that you feel completely overwhelmed or 'dis-abled' by them, then the 'call to action' may be to give yourself permission to seek support and if genuinely needed, to seek independent professional support in talking things through to help to identify the most appropriate way forwards.

New York Times bestselling Author Katherine Woodward Thomas uses the term, *'Inner Detective'*. I love this language.

When we notice, we immediately create the possibility of becoming an observer of our own experience.

We create the possibility of becoming our own inner detective: the investigator (and therefore the solver) of our problems.

Mindfulness Meets Emotional Awareness

When our mind notices our emotions with enquiry and interest, compassion and care, combined with knowledge of our individual emotional states, we can begin to unravel the nature of the information they are bringing us and to use this to inform the choices and the decisions that we face within our lives on a daily basis.

In the next Chapter, we will begin our exploration of each of our most challenging emotions.

"If you don't manage your emotions, your emotions will manage you."

Doc Childre and Deborah Rozman, from *Transforming Anxiety*

Mindfulness Meets Emotional Awareness

Chapter 1

Healthy Fear and Healthy Anxiety

"You're not human if you don't feel fear.
But I've learned to treat fear as an emotion that sharpens me.
It's there to give me that edge for what I have to do."

Edward Michael "Bear" Grylls (b. 1974), adventurer, writer
and television presenter

For my first chapter in my exploration of our most
challenging emotions I am going to dive in at the deep end.

Let's talk about fear and anxiety. This is a biggie!

Fear is a powerful emotional driver. When we are afraid or
anxious, these emotions color our perceptions and views
thereby influencing and potentially altering our decisions, our
choices and our actions. And this has an impact on us, not
only as individuals within the scope of our own personal and
family lives, but also within our wider social groups, our
communities and on a national and global scale.

**Left unchecked, fear can spread like a virus, obliterating all
reason and as such it is an emotion that lends itself well to
misrepresentation and misuse.**

Sadly, this is an emotion that has been readily used as an effective weapon to instigate and justify acts of atrocity, violence, hatred, inequality and prejudice; many a war has been instigated by the use of fear, artfully channeled to fuel a tide of emotive reaction.

Even within societies that consider themselves sophisticated and well educated, we see and hear fear being used to influence and maneuver. Within our families and within our communities, within our schools, and within the workplace, instances of bullying can readily be found, with fear being used as an effective weapon not only against individuals or groups that are being targeted, but also in controlling those who know that this kind of behavior is wrong, but have become fearful of saying anything for fear of being targeted themselves.

It is hardly surprising then that many people view both fear and indeed anxiety as some kind of an enemy.

In truth, however, these powerful emotions do have a purpose.

Our ability to handle these feelings, our understanding of them, our relationship with them, and therefore what we do in response to them, will make the difference between these emotions feeling like an asset or a disability.

Mindfulness Meets Emotional Awareness

Our capacity to remain calm and mindful of our choices in the tsunami of an intensely fearful emotional experience will make the difference between fear becoming the instigator of positive and valuable outcomes within our lives, generating safety and significant growth and awareness, or of fear becoming critically disabling, never quite leaving us, and causing ongoing longer-term challenges.

In over 26 years of therapeutic practice I have met more people suffering from issues stemming from some kind of fear or anxiety, than from any other of our more challenging emotions.

While fear and anxiety are related, they serve us in very different ways and it will pay us to understand this difference, particularly if we are to overcome any kind of ongoing problems associated with these emotions.

It is also helpful to differentiate between 'healthy fear' and 'healthy anxiety' as opposed to 'unhealthy' or 'inappropriate' fear and anxiety.

So, let's talk about healthy fear.

In its primary capacity, fear brings us the gift of protection, and therefore the gift of safety.

Now, this may seem an extreme contradiction to our actual experience of fear, because when we feel fear, we don't feel safe... we don't feel safe at all! But when we feel fear, it is actually informing us of a lack of safety.

41

Healthy fear is an immediate and fully present experience. It is a response to something that is happening right here and right now. When we experience a genuine and real threat, it is absolutely essential that we listen to our fear and we take action!

If I were out walking and a car careered off the road, my healthy fear would activate immediately and, fueled by adrenaline, I would get out of the way. Without fear, self-preservation would be absent.

When a pride of lions sets out to hunt, the animals they are hunting immediately move into high alert. They experience fear, and this is appropriate.

However, when the hunt is over and fear is no longer needed, they turn their alert system back down again, and within a very short space of time, they will be grazing as normal, often not far from the pride of lions who just half an hour previously were an immediate and very real danger.

The threat is over and they are continuing with their lives.

They do not constantly look over their shoulders anticipating the next attack, never relaxing and never recovering from the ordeal.

Nor are they living in a state of denial, dissociated from fear in a way that renders it inactive, leaving them vulnerable to attack when the lions next set out to hunt.

Mindfulness Meets Emotional Awareness

As human being's we are different. One of the difficulties that we can run into in our relationship with fear is that we often lack the skills to self-regulate its intensity and its duration. When we experience fear we don't necessarily turn the volume of our high alert system back down automatically. Once our fear has been activated, even though the threat is over and the same situation may be highly unlikely to ever happen again, we go over and over it in our mind, unable to shake it off and put it behind us.

This leads me nicely to anxiety.

Whilst anxiety and fear are connected, they are not the same.

Healthy anxiety is an emotional state that sits in relationship with both fear and excitement. If we were to put fear and excitement at either end of a line, healthy anxiety sits somewhere in the middle, and it serves a very important purpose.

If we are encountering something unknown and new for the first time, appropriate anxiety focuses our attention, it turns up our alert system just a little, so we have a heightened level of concentration. It gives us an edge, and in a new and unknown situation this is helpful.

Likewise, when we approach something that we know is going to be challenging, our healthy anxiety before the event informs us to prepare, as well as giving us that edge when we come to face that challenge in the present moment.

When we sit in healthy relationship with anxiety, a challenging situation can become a stretch and something to grow into, rather than a stress and something to be feared.

Mindfulness Meets Emotional Awareness

So healthy anxiety, like healthy fear, is an immediate and fully present experience, however it is also an emotion that can serve us ahead of time.

This emotional state of heightened awareness combined with reflective and grounded thought creates an opportunity for preparation. The key here is the combination of heightened awareness grounded in pragmatic thought.

In our everyday lives, when we engage in any kind of activity that contains an element of risk, however big or small, it's our healthy awareness of fear with appropriate levels of anxiety in combination with the reflective capacity of our mind that informs us. The emotional element of our awareness in response to a potential hazard or danger affords us the opportunity to take mindful and considered precautionary measures.

If we work, or play, in an environment that involves risk, we mindfully put safety measures in place to support our actions.

When we teach our children to look both ways before they cross the road, we are teaching them about healthy fear and healthy anxiety. When, where, and how these emotions are appropriate, and what action to take.

Caution is an outcome of healthy, appropriate fear and anxiety and a very good example of our mind and our emotions collaborating and working together as a team.

Why and when do fear and anxiety become unhealthy?

Mindfulness Meets Emotional Awareness

A good starting point is to differentiate between the kind of fear that is felt in the immediacy of a moment, when a threat is very real and very present such as being involved in an accident, or being under any form of genuine threat, as opposed to the kinds of fears that we hold within us and within our mind, such as fear of the unknown, fear of failure, fear of catastrophe and disaster, fear of abandonment, of loss and death… the list is endless.

The difference sits in 'the fear of what might be' as opposed to 'the fear of what is'.

'The fear of what might be' is often at the root of ongoing problems of anxiety. While these kinds of fears are in many ways completely natural and are very much part of being human, the purpose they need to serve is to heighten our capacity to think about ourselves in ways that anticipate challenges in realistic ways, helping us to prepare for and to navigate difficult or new and unknown situations.

When we identify possible problems, we can identify possible solutions. This is a valuable life skill! Likewise, if we have to face a genuinely threatening situation any anxiety or fear ahead of time should be informing our decision making as to how we approach this situation.

However, there is a world of difference between an active, creative mind seeking solutions and outcomes that fuel inner confidence and generate emotional resilience and self-worth, and the kind of negative, repetitive thoughts of impending catastrophe that create an ever increasing and endless cycle of potential crisis and disaster!

Mindfulness Meets Emotional Awareness

These kinds of thoughts generate self-doubt, reducing our confidence and our self-worth and they play a significant part in anxiety-related procrastination.

I call these thoughts 'The What If Thoughts' and they come under the umbrella of what I have come to refer to as **Repetitive Thought Syndrome.**

Repetitive Thought Syndrome is an internal dialogue within our mind that once activated tends to follow a repeating pattern.

I have noticed that the storylines played out in these repetitive thought patterns tend to follow common themes depending on the specific emotion that is driving them and with fear and anxiety the theme is made up of 'What If' scenarios of impending catastrophe and disaster!

Whilst these thoughts stem from fear and anxiety, they also generate more of the same!

'What If' scenarios create a constant underlying edge of ongoing anxiety which in effect is fueling and feeding itself. Left unchecked, these thoughts have the potential to spiral into a state of heightened stress and extreme high alert.

Every 'What If' situation is imagined with a series of potentially negative or disastrous outcomes which in turn fuel further 'What If' scenarios to try and anticipate all eventualities. As storylines unfold within our minds, each scenario creating even more fear and further imagined and impending crisis, rather than fueling confidence and building decision-making skills they do the opposite!

Eventually, so much fear is generated that every decision we face can be perceived as a disaster waiting to happen. Any form of basic trust is undermined, especially trust in ourselves. Self-confidence diminishes, fueling self-doubt, uncertainty and unease, creating extremely low self-esteem with an ongoing susceptibility to high anxiety.

(Additional Resources 1. The Difference between Confidence and Self-Esteem. Audio. © Jenny Burgess A-Z of Emotional Health on-line Library, a free on-line resource http://bit.ly/2sY9ajY)

If we were to place this state of heightened worry and concern on a sliding scale in a red, amber, green alert system, with red being high alert, and green being a state of complete relaxation, people who live with this level of ongoing fear and anxiety very rarely relax into a state of green.

They tend to sit at the high end of amber fluctuating easily to red, and their underlying anxiety never quite lets up. This inability to fully relax has massive implications for our health and well-being both physically and mentally.

So why do some people feel this way and others not?

There are a variety of reasons that support our understanding of this and no doubt as science and the exploration of our mind continues, we will come to know even more. Whilst there will of course be unique and individual circumstances in play, I have found two underlying common denominators that seem to consistently underpin issues related to fear and anxiety.

Sensitivity and Trauma

Firstly sensitivity. It is useful to recognize that some people are by nature of a more sensitive disposition than others. This is not a criticism of those who are sensitive, nor indeed of those who are not, simply a helpful piece of information to be aware of and acknowledge. I am sure we can all think of situations or scenarios in which one person can take something deeply to heart whilst another might seem relatively oblivious and untouched by it.

As a generalized rule, I have found that people who experience anxiety-related problems are of an extremely sensitive nature.

Now whilst sensitivity is a marvelous gift, it can also have a bit of a double edge to it. People who are highly sensitive tend to pick up on any emotional undercurrents around them; like a sponge they have an emotional absorbency and will sense any underlying uneasiness and tension around them.

In its positive form, this can give them an edge and a wonderfully heightened sensitivity to others. However, the downside to this is that it can also leave them vulnerable, easily bruised and lacking in emotional durability.

In my experience if you are of a sensitive nature you will need to learn to manage your sensitivity.

Secondly if we are struggling with any form of inappropriate fear or anxiety, we need to consider the existence of any historic trauma that we may carry within us.

Mindfulness Meets Emotional Awareness

In the format of this book I cannot possibly do justice to the scope and enormity of this subject, however I need to at least give us a reference point to begin our understanding of the impact of traumatic experiences on anxiety and fear related problems.

I am going to define trauma as the emotional outcome or emotional consequence that comes from an experience of something happening to us that is out of our control. We are helpless and unable to do anything about it, frightened or even terrified and we lose all sense of safety.

We tend to think of trauma in relation to big and catastrophic events, but there are in fact many different types and levels of trauma. Some are apparent and known about and some are not!

In considering problems related to fear and anxiety, it is valuable to be aware of both 'known trauma' and 'unknown trauma.'

If we experience a big event, such as an accident, any form of violation or abuse, or we are witness to something horrific, this is a *known trauma*. Depending on the nature and the extent of these experiences because the origins of the trauma are known about, the symptoms that we experience have a context and even though our emotions will be unbelievably challenging we will at least have some kind of an understanding as to why we feel the way that we do and therefore, providing we are in an emotionally responsive environment, the potential to allow ourselves the opportunity to seek help and to receive some kind of support.

Often the biggest challenge in these kinds of circumstances is to feel okay about asking for help. Sadly, we still live in a culture where within certain social groups, showing any form of emotional vulnerability is interpreted as a weakness, especially in men.

This needs to change!

We can also experience forms of trauma that are *unknown*.

If we experience any form of trauma when we are very tiny, either before we have reached an age where we can have a clear memory of what took place or before we were old enough for our circumstances to be explained to us by the adults around us in a way that would make the world feel safe again, then although we will still carry the impact of that traumatic experience within us, we will have no conscious recollection of what actually took place or of its full impact on us.

We therefore have no reference point or context to give us an understanding of why we feel the way that we do.

We also now know that we can experience forms of *inherited trauma*.

Cutting-edge epigenetic research has shown that trauma can be passed down through generations at a cellular level. The outcome of this is that some people will find themselves with a predisposition to having a traumatic emotional response to certain triggers without necessarily knowing how or why they feel this way.

Mindfulness Meets Emotional Awareness

To have a powerful emotional response without any understanding of why we feel this way is traumatic in itself, as it leaves us feeling as though we ourselves are out of our own control.

(Additional Resources 2. Recommended further reading. Super Genes. Deepak Chopra, M.D. and Rudolph Tanzi, Ph.D. http://amzn.to/2uI2v0M)

I have also come across a particularly powerful form of unknown trauma that develops as a direct result of relational isolation.

In many ways, it isn't so much that it is unknown, but more that it is unrecognized. When I speak about this with people, I refer to it as *relational trauma*.

We are primarily relational beings and our capacity to feel okay about ourselves and to develop emotional resilience is dependent upon us receiving an appropriate level of relational responsiveness from others.

Put simply, to be emotionally healthy we need to feel understood and related to by others.

If we are isolated or alone in a difficult situation with no-one to reach out to for support, then our inner feelings of helplessness will generate high levels of stress and anxiety.

If these feelings continue and are left unattended to, with no respite (and therefore no underlying return to a place of inner safety or relaxation), then slowly but surely, we will move into a state of high alert.

Mindfulness Meets Emotional Awareness

For anyone growing up in a world of emotional isolation this ongoing state of high alert will have been 'the norm' and is therefore frequently not recognized. The trauma of unrelatedness tends to evolve slowly over a long period of time.

Living with an ongoing experience of heightened stress and emotional challenge creates a significant predisposition to being affected adversely by fear and anxiety in later life, potentially triggered in any moment.

When unprocessed this type of unrecognized relational trauma has a massive impact on the development of our self-esteem and self-worth and in our ability to develop trust. And as such, is frequently at the root of many relationship problems and relational insecurities.

Relational trauma can also be present in the form of a what I term a *'secondary trauma'*.

If, in the aftermath of a traumatic incident, we do not receive the necessary support and validation that we need in order to work through and process our experience, then already traumatized by a primary event the lack of an appropriate response creates a further trauma in itself and as such it generates a secondary level of trauma.

I have come across victims of rape and abuse who in trying to seek support were either disbelieved or even worse found themselves the target of blame. The lack of a thoughtful and sensitive response in the form of either denial or accusation was in itself, a further traumatic event.

Many anxiety-related problems have their roots in some form of trauma, either known or unknown and sometimes in a combination of both.

In any form of trauma, the scars that remain are inevitably the emotional ones and these will need to be processed, in order to put them down and place them firmly in the past where they belong.

The way to heal any aspect of relational trauma is through an experience of healthy relationship where a consistent and reliable response will over time repair and replace the memory of previous experience.

If any form of trauma is significant and its effects long lasting this is often best responded to in relationship with an appropriate professional.

If you are struggling with any form of anxiety, never be afraid to seek the support that you need and should you initially find an inappropriate response or simply not gel with that particular person, then please look further afield.

My invitation for today

Today I wish to invite you to learn to identify the difference between healthy, appropriate fear and anxiety and unhealthy, inappropriate fear and anxiety and to develop some skills in managing these emotions.

My thought for today

"Turn down the volume and don't double the load!"

A useful exercise

This is a very simple exercise, but extremely helpful in learning to turn down the volume on any ongoing anxiety that we may be experiencing.

In the introduction, I spoke about the way in which we can double our emotional load. This can happen with many of our emotions, however it is a particularly common experience with fear and anxiety. If we have ever experienced any kind of intense fear or anxiety then, understandably, we can become fearful of feeling these emotions again.

When we find ourselves challenged by these strong and overwhelming emotions, our feelings can be so intense that we can feel as though we ourselves are out of our own control especially if we are dealing with the residue of any form of trauma. This in itself then tends to generate further anxiety and fear about the way that we're feeling.
We literally become fearful... of feeling fearful!

Mindfulness Meets Emotional Awareness

The moment we experience any kind of nervousness or anxiety, even if it's a completely appropriate and natural reaction to our current circumstances, we are so afraid of being overwhelmed by these feelings again that we immediately move into a state of heightened anxiety about the way that we are feeling.

When we are 'fearful of feeling fearful' we have just doubled the emotional load!

When we are fearful of the way that we feel, we are creating a secondary package of emotion on top of an already challenging emotional experience. Having a major wobble when we are already wobbling is unhelpful. We really don't need to make ourselves feel even worse!

The key to changing this lies in our ability to learn to press a pause button: to notice and to listen without adding further anxiety or fear to the mix and to re-evaluate our situation from a position of considered choice.

Because both fear and anxiety are connected to feelings of being out of control, one of the most empowering responses is to evaluate where we are, right here and right now, and to take charge of the possible responses and choices over which we do actually have control.

There is a direct relationship between choice and the recovery from trauma.

(Additional Resources 3. Further reading. Huffington Post Blog. Why our Right to Choose Keeps Us Healthy. © Jenny Florence 2015 http://huff.to/29kHxdA)

Mindfulness Meets Emotional Awareness

I know that for myself, whenever I am experiencing any kind of anxiety or repetitive thinking, I will need to have a grounding conversation with myself.

An inner dialogue that will allow me to clarify what's going on and help me to put down any unhelpful thoughts that might be contributing to my anxiety, before I then consider my options and my choices.

Even if I'm facing challenging circumstances and the choices available to me are not the choices that I would like, I know that my opportunity for choice does still exist and identifying and clarifying my options will stop my emotions from spiraling.

Make some time and space in which you will not be disturbed. We are going to check in with ourselves, ground our thoughts and consider our choices.

Before we begin let's remind ourselves of the extraordinary wisdom of the serenity prayer by the American theologian Reinhold Niebuhr:

"God, grant me the serenity to accept the things I cannot change,

Courage to change the things I can,

And the wisdom to know the difference."

Using your journal or some paper, write a list of any concerns, fears and worries that you are dwelling on and then answer the following questions:

Mindfulness Meets Emotional Awareness

- Do your current fears and worries fears fall under the category of - the 'Fear of What Is' or of - the 'Fear of What Might Be'?
- Are you experiencing any 'What If' patterns of thinking? If so what are they?
- Is your response to these thoughts and feelings reassuring, calming and soothing or is it critical and anxiety-provoking, adding fuel to the fire and causing you greater worry?
- Are you anxious about the way that you feel? Are you doubling the load?

Now differentiate between any situations that genuinely need attending to, as opposed to those that are hypothetical.

Unless these 'Might Be' scenarios are going to need valid attention or constitute a genuinely constructive element in clarifying your choices, please give yourself permission to put them down along with any related 'What If' thoughts.

Write them down and then in whatever way feels right for you, physically let go of them. Put them in a blank envelope and post them, or burn them (safely!), or put them out with the rubbish.

The act of identifying these thoughts and feelings whilst giving absolute permission to let go of them in such a physical way is extremely therapeutic.

Repeat this as often as you need to.

Now take any fears and anxieties about 'What Actually Is' or 'What Definitely Will' need attending to and answer the following questions:

Mindfulness Meets Emotional Awareness

- Are you in any kind of immediate threat or danger?
- If you are, what do you need to do right now and who can you reach out to for help?
- If you are not in any immediate threat or danger, but are nevertheless in a genuinely challenging situation, then your feelings are there to inform and assist you in making considered choices.

Take some time to explore your choices and options.

- What is within your power to change, and what is not?
- How can you use these feelings to inform your preparation?
- Who can you turn to for help and support, or simply to talk through your feelings and concerns? - This question can present us with a major challenge if we are feeling isolated or alone. In considering who to turn to I would wish to include support that is beyond our immediate family and friends. Please include on-line forums, local support groups and any professional support networks in your area.

Write a list of the realistic choices and options that are available to you, as well as a list of the support networks around you that you may want to call on for further support in taking action.

If your anxiety or fear is so extreme in intensity that you feel completely overwhelmed or 'dis-abled' then the healthiest choice may be to give yourself permission to seek independent professional support in talking things through to help to identify the most appropriate way forwards.

Mindfulness Meets Emotional Awareness

Even when the choices available to us are not those that we would actually like or indeed want for ourselves, there is almost always a choice that we can take.

When we learn to listen to ourselves and take responsibility for our own choices, including learning from any mistakes along the way, then regardless of our circumstances we will find the opportunity for change and to sow the seeds of empowerment within ourselves.

"Highly sensitive people are too often perceived as weaklings or damaged goods.
To feel intensely is not a symptom of weakness, it is the trademark of the truly alive and compassionate. It is not the empath who is broken, it is society that has become dysfunctional and emotionally disabled.
There is no shame in expressing your authentic feelings.
Those who are at times described as being a 'hot mess' or having 'too many issues' are the very fabric of what keeps the dream alive for a more caring, humane world.
Never be ashamed to let your tears shine a light in this world."

Anthon St. Maarten. Coach and Spiritual Author

Mindfulness Meets Emotional Awareness

Chapter 2

Healthy Shame and Guilt

"Hard though it may be to accept, remember that guilt is sometimes a friendly internal voice reminding you that you're messing up."

Marge Kennedy (b. 1896), English novelist and playwright

We all mess up sometimes… it's part of being a normal human being.

What we do about it and whether we see a mistake as a valuable learning curve, or as a crisis, will be influenced by our understanding and our attitude towards the underlying feelings that we experience when we get something wrong.

Shame and guilt are notoriously perceived as bad and negative and yet in truth they are both core emotional components in our capacity to develop self-reflection and self-regulation.

One of the biggest problems that we face, both within the immediacy of our own communities as well as on a global scale, are the actions of people who possess a lack of either of these emotions.

Without guilt and without shame we have no conscience. Fundamentally, the role of these important emotions is to support us in developing our self-responsibility.

The benefits of both shame and guilt are that they enable us to become decent human beings. They enable us to live with care and with consideration, mindful of the consequences of our actions with a level of concern and regard that stops us from hurting others.

Curiously enough, it is frequently those who are lacking in the integration of these emotions within their personality who, without experiencing any form of remorse, use them to manipulate and maneuver others.

Sadly, these are emotions that are easily misused. The most significant problems arising from the misuse of guilt and shame are situations where these emotions are used as weapons, either against others — or indeed as a weapon against ourselves.

The healthy role of both shame and guilt is one of self-control, not in the control of others!

The healthy role of both shame and guilt is one of self-regulation, not self-persecution!

These emotions are here to support our personal awareness of the impact of our actions on both ourselves as well as others and in our personal awareness of the impact of the actions of others.

Shame and guilt are both emotions of relational awareness and given that we are fundamentally relational beings, are profoundly important to us.

Mindfulness Meets Emotional Awareness

As a diagnostic tool in our emotional toolbox they enable us to develop both personal responsibility and discernment, in relation to our own actions as well as in response to the actions of others.

Guilt and shame are often spoken about in the same breath and we will often find a connection between the two, they can certainly feed and fuel each other and both may trigger similar responses from us; they are however fundamentally quite different.

When we feel shame, the focus is singular and within ourselves. When we feel shame or indeed when we are 'made' to feel shame, it is as though we have let ourselves down. We feel mortified and wish that the ground would swallow us up. Shame is colored by embarrassment and the potential for personal humiliation.

When we feel guilt, the emphasis of our concern is that we have caused a problem or difficulty to another, our emotional focus is in our awareness of the other person. We feel mortified that we have hurt someone else and may well feel driven to put this right.

To be able to use these emotions effectively it is helpful to identify and develop our understanding of the most common problems that we experience from both shame and guilt, while simultaneously identifying solutions and ways of approaching these challenging emotions from a different perspective.

Let's first talk about shame.

Mindfulness Meets Emotional Awareness

When we make a mistake, or we get something wrong and we feel shame, the spotlight is turned on ourselves, so shame holds a singular, self-focused experience. The benefit of this is it enables us to monitor and self-regulate our actions.

Shame supports us in learning from our mistakes.

When shame results in a process of self-reflection in which we learn from the experience, it has served its purpose. Shame is not an emotion that should be carried around as a burden.

If we have addressed a problem and genuinely done all that we can to actively seek a resolution, then regardless of the outcome we have every right to feel good about ourselves. This kind of response to shame should alleviate our feelings and promote self-worth.

When our responsiveness to shame generates and adds to a foundation of healthy self-esteem, the experience will be relatively short lived.

If we have genuinely done something wrong, but can forgive ourselves and take whatever action is necessary to address the problem, and know that it is a lesson learned and that we have no intention of making the same mistake again then beyond being a memory, shame should remain with us only as long as it takes us to process the experience.

Forgiveness is key in our ability to process shame in a way that promotes our personal awareness and growth and contributes to the development of a healthy personality.

Sadly, however, shame is an emotional state that is easily and frequently misused.

Mindfulness Meets Emotional Awareness

Shame generates our concern about the way that we are seen, by others and by society in general, and as such it has a function in our ability to become a part of a community and to learn the requirements of 'the tribe'. It is therefore a powerful influence on our ability to feel as though we belong.

Sadly, it is exactly this function of being a part of something and our primary need to belong that opens it up to be so easily misused! Colored by embarrassment and with the potential for humiliation, when forgiveness and understanding are absent, indeed when they are harnessed as justification, shame can become a powerful tool for manipulation.

I recently attended a talk by Jasvinda Sanghera.

(Additional Resources 4. Further reading. Jasvinda Sanghera. Shame. http://amzn.to/2uFNcq7 *).*

In her book *Shame,* she speaks of her own personal experience where, as a teenager, she ran away from home to avoid an imposed marriage to a man that she had never met. She describes in accurate and distressing detail the way in which shame is misused in the name of 'family respect' and 'family honor'.

Let me be very clear! There is neither respect nor honor in any action that violates the healthy choice of another. Nor is there any respect or honor in an action that rides on the use of fear as a form of control and is devoid of either care or compassion.

Mindfulness Meets Emotional Awareness

The intentional manipulation and violation of the rights and entitlement to make decisions for ourselves with our personal choice respected, demonstrates an absolute lack of remorse and therefore a lack of either shame or guilt on the part of the enforcer.

It is a tragedy that the victims of such manipulations are left with extreme feelings of shame and the perpetrator devoid of any!

Whenever any form of violation of another is presented as justifiable, whether we justify it to ourselves or to others, this avoidance and denial of the damaging and destructive impact of our actions highlights an absence of conscience.

People who avoid shame through justification are unlikely to learn from their mistakes in ways that will inform and regulate their future actions with an awareness of the possible consequences. Whereas people who experience shame in the face of a genuine mistake and are able to take appropriate reparative action, will learn from their mistakes and indeed grow from their mistakes, transforming their experiences into knowledge and wisdom. This in turn fuels a healthy level of self-respect and genuine self-esteem.

By learning from our mistakes, we feel good about ourselves!

When we have an 'ownership' of both shame and guilt, and we use this 'good information' to inform us and to fuel our personal growth and learning, any residue of these emotions will dissipate. When we are unable to make sense of either shame or guilt and to use them as part of a natural and valuable learning curve, they will remain with us.

Mindfulness Meets Emotional Awareness

Both shame and guilt can weigh heavily on our shoulders and whilst in essence, they are different, they often accompany one another.

Finding a resolution to these emotional states alleviates their burden.

Let us now consider guilt.

Guilt is a different experience from that of shame. When we make a mistake, or get something wrong, guilt is the emotion that generates concern about others. We feel guilty because we realize that our actions have had a detrimental impact on another.

From a developmental point of view, when we arrive at a position of experiencing guilt, then we have moved forwards enough in life to have developed an awareness and a concern for the well-being of others.

Our attention, our focus, and our core concern is no longer singular. Our concern stretches to more than ourselves and we feel uncomfortable and concerned when our actions have caused hurt or damage to someone or something else.

Guilt is the extraordinary emotion that enables us to develop a conscience and to be concerned about others and about the world beyond ourselves.

Mindfulness Meets Emotional Awareness

Interestingly our capacity to experience guilt is a central component in our ability to develop empathy. To become empathic and aware of the feelings of others, we need to be able to experience guilt without being overwhelmed or disabled by it.

Clearly consideration and a regard for others is a lovely quality and one we would all wish to see more of in the world — it demonstrates that we care — but for those who possess it in excess and without an appropriate level of assessment or discernment, the burden of guilt can lead to an inappropriate over-giving, often at the expense of oneself.
This can also create an area of particular vulnerability when dealing with people who are looking for others to meet their needs and who lack the ability or indeed the desire to be responsible for themselves.

Sadly, guilt is an emotion that lends itself well as a punitive tool for manipulation.

A skilled manipulator will use it to maneuver and control others with great effect and used in this way it can leave a caring individual feeling an inappropriate and excessive level of responsibility for the happiness or well-being of others.

I have also met people who are absolutely crippled by guilt, not necessarily being put upon them by others but in effect being used as a weapon of restriction and limitation by themselves… against themselves.

If you happen to fall into the category of over-caring, then firstly let me say thank you: the world needs people who care!

Mindfulness Meets Emotional Awareness

However, let's be very real about this. There will always be a reason or some history involved as to why we become over-givers in the first place.

Our desire to help and make a difference is in one way wonderful, however it can also be some sort of compensation for something within ourselves that we have yet to attend to. Over-giving or inappropriate giving can also have its roots in feelings of guilt and obligation.

None of us should be forced to give out of either guilt or obligation, whether imposed by others or by ourselves. Healthy giving is born of love and authentic desire.

For the well-being of everyone it is essential that over-givers and over-carers learn to manage these qualities in themselves. Ultimately, we do nobody any favors by giving too much at the expense of ourselves.

When we over-give, the takers of the world remain dependent without the opportunity to really step up and discover their own potential and the over-givers will inevitably burn out or develop deep seated resentments at carrying such a burden.

Whenever I meet an 'over-giver' and we begin to discuss issues of self-care I like to use the analogy of a jug of water. If you are constantly filling up everyone else's cup without pausing to refill your own, then sooner or later you will run dry!

As a rule of thumb, if primarily we take care of ourselves, we will have an abundance to give and to share with others.

Mindfulness Meets Emotional Awareness

It is valuable to keep this in mind in situations where we find ourselves saying Yes, when really, we should be saying No, particularly if either guilt or shame is present in the exchange.

(Additional Resources 5. A Meditation. The Art of Saying Yes and Saying No. © Jenny Burgess A-Z of Emotional Health on-line Library, a free on-line resource http://bit.ly/2r6cVX0) 'Over-givers' also frequently possess a kind of heightened sensitivity and absorbency of the emotional states of those around them, with an instinctive need to try to put things right and to keep everyone happy.

If you are an over-giver you may need to give yourself permission to consciously place self-care at the top of your agenda.

Whether it is in the development of discernment and an awareness of our own giving, or in our awareness of guilt or shame being used to coerce us into complying with the wishes of others, it will serve us well to develop our awareness of the underlying emotional exchanges that take place in our relational interactions.

This level of awareness can keep us grounded and help us to maintain healthy boundaries with others as well as with ourselves.

In every exchange that takes place between us there are many layers of communication and whether it's an event or a verbal communication, there will always be some kind of underlying emotional exchange taking place, like an emotional currency being passed between us and guilt and shame are passed easily within these exchanges.

If I were to give a gift to somebody, and I give it freely with joy, love and appreciation, then when they receive that gift, they will also receive the emotional gift. They will receive the emotional package of joy and love and appreciation. It will feel good!

However, if I were to give the same gift to somebody, but I gave it out of guilt, obligation and duty, then even though the event may appear to be exactly the same, the emotional package that comes with it will create a completely different exchange. No joy is present, and they will have to deal with the underlying unease present in the exchange. It won't feel the same and it certainly won't feel good!

Let's say that I were then to give the very same gift to somebody, but I chose to do so because I had an ulterior motive, a plan in mind, so that at a later date, I could call in a favor. Like scoring brownie points in advance, a gesture given, knowing full well that I intend to maneuver somebody into a position at a later date where they would feel obliged to give me what I want.

The gift may appear to be delightful, however the emotional package that comes with it is absolutely loaded!

The outcome of this kind of exchange will be determined by the awareness of the receiver and of their ability to process, to know, and to understand what is actually being given to them before deciding whether or not to accept the gift.

Mindfulness Meets Emotional Awareness

To a very great extent their ability to choose whether to say either Yes or No appropriately will depend upon their ability to recognize what is actually going on and their ability to recognize the underlying emotional currency — and this will depend upon their ability to recognize and relate to their own emotional experience.

Developing this kind of internal healthy assessment strengthens our trust in our ability to make decisions that self-regulate our actions and foster healthy relationships, with an appropriate level of personal discernment. This in turn builds and maintains both our self-confidence and our self-esteem.

When we are able to listen to ourselves without judgement or retribution and with forgiveness and appreciation, both shame and guilt become key players in the evolution of our self-awareness and our personal growth.

Mindfulness Meets Emotional Awareness

My invitation for today

Today I wish like to invite you to process guilt and shame and turn them into positive learning.

My thought for today

**"A mistake is a valuable learning curve,
not a burden to be held on to and carried for life."**

Wisdom and maturity are not marked by our years, they are marked by our ability to learn from our mistakes and to integrate this learning into our future actions. For this to take place, we will need to welcome both shame and guilt with interest, curiosity and a desire to grow.

We have acknowledged that both guilt and shame are emotions of relational exchange.

In very simplistic terms, whether in circumstance or relationship something has gone wrong and we feel 'bad' about it.

Much of the challenge that we face with these emotions comes from their misuse, or our inability to process them appropriately in ways that allows us to let go and to move forwards and to be at peace with ourselves.

A useful exercise

Mindfulness Meets Emotional Awareness

The diagram at the end of this chapter highlights the kinds of behavior and responses that are associated with the wide spectrum of both of these powerful emotions, with too much guilt and shame at one end of the scale and not enough at the other!

It is designed to serve as a useful guideline or reference point in considering any situation that involves either of these powerful emotions. It is also available to download and print from the A-Z of Emotional health on-line Library.

Neither end of the spectrum holds a position of health. Ideally, we wish to sit in a balanced position where we take considered responsible action without being 'held responsible for' or indeed 'holding ourselves responsible for' the issues of another.

If you are finding yourself challenged by either shame or guilt, let me invite you to engage your inner detective and use these extraordinary emotions to inform you.

Centre yourself in a position grounded in compassion and care. Bring your attention to yourself and take some time to identify the circumstances that have caused these feelings.

If we have indeed made a mistake, or our actions have resulted in a problem then these emotions are a call to action to address the issue in hand. If the circumstances are legitimate then these emotions create the opportunity to say sorry, to make amends and to put something right.

Ask yourself: 'what actions can I take to address and resolve the situation'?

In this instance write a list of all your possible choices in terms of seeking a resolution. Notice any other emotions that are present and use them to inform your choices.

Now take action.

If an apology is not well received then ask yourself: 'have I done everything that I can to resolve the situation'?

If this is the case, then I would ask you to consider letting go of any ongoing feelings of guilt or shame.

When we can put our hand on our heart and know that we did all that we could to address the problem, then neither guilt nor shame should remain with us. The inability to forgive and to move on is not our problem to carry.

The value of these emotions is to learn from them, not to carry them with us in eternal retribution!

If our feelings are a reference to something that we did in the past, something that we cannot change or put right, then the call to action is one of reflection and of learning. We cannot change our past actions, but we can choose not to do the same again.

Casting your mind back, what have you learned from the situation and how can you apply this to future events and relationships?

Write a list of the valuable life lessons gained from the situation. If appropriate, take action.

Give yourself positive feedback and healthy validation for your honesty and for your desire to learn and to grow.

Are your feelings in the scenario fueled by either fear or obligation?

If our feelings have their origins in fear and the circumstances are of obligation, then their underlying motives demand some further investigation.

This is a powerful call to action.

Take time to reflect on the situation. Think very carefully about the implications of your own actions as well as the actions of any others involved in the scenario. Use the diagram provided as a frame of reference to help you to identify the various positions of all parties involved.

Many problems in the world stem from the actions of people who lack guilt and shame, and have no remorse!

Others sit at the opposite end of the spectrum, carrying more far more of these emotions than their fair share, often burdened and held back by this overload. There is an imbalance.

Ask yourself: 'are these feelings of either guilt or shame presenting me with a conflict between my own well-being and the desires of others'?

Sometimes, particularly if we lean heavily towards the overwhelming/over-giving end of the spectrum it can be a challenge to put our own well-being above that of others.

Mindfulness Meets Emotional Awareness

Return to the diagram again to help you to find clarity as to the various positions of all parties involved, especially yourself.

For an over-giver, the healthy action is to take time to reflect on what kind of support you may need to enhance your capacity for discernment and to firm up your boundaries and perceptions of what constitutes healthy giving.

Sometimes our feelings of both shame and guilt are connected to a past situation over which we had no control whatsoever.

This is a common occurrence following any kind of abuse or trauma, particularly during childhood when we simply didn't know enough to realize that what was happening to us was not our fault or indeed, our responsibility.

In this kind of scenario, we can find ourselves revisiting a situation again and again questioning why it happened or if we could have done something to prevent what took place. This is a very natural response. However, if this is the case, then the appropriate course of action is to seek support. We have every right to be supported in learning to process our experiences and to lay the past to rest.

Remaining emotionally attached to a situation over which we had no control simply because it lies in the past will not serve us in any way.

The healthy role of both shame and guilt is one of self-regulation and as such they are actually core components of self-reflection.

Mindfulness Meets Emotional Awareness

When these powerful emotions are integrated into our understanding without fear or judgement, they offer us the opportunity to monitor both our actions and the actions of others around us.

This enables us to develop healthy discernment built on a foundation of strong boundaries; boundaries that establish and consolidate our core inner values and the way in which we express these values within our immediate relationships, in our communities and in the world at large.

"We are dangerous when we are not conscious of our responsibility for how we behave, think, and feel."

Marshall B. Rosenberg (b. 1934), American psychologist and developer of non-violent communication.

Diagram 1

Absence of Shame & Guilt		Overwhelming Shame & Guilt
No Guilt. No Shame.	**A Good Relationship with both Guilt and Shame.**	**Overbearing sense of Guilt and Shame.**
Demonstrates a lack of conscience and a lack of care.	Perceives mistakes as a valuable learning curve.	Overly Self-critical.
Inability to apologize without remorse if others are hurt by their actions.	Understands the difference between a critic and a critique!	Often say Yes when you would prefer to say No.
An inability to learn from one's own mistakes.	Welcomes reflective feedback with enquiry and interest.	Put others first even at the expense of yourself.
A lack of self-responsibility.	Can say both Yes and No with respect for oneself and others.	Low self-esteem.
Readily blames others.	Demonstrates empathy and an ability to listen, not only to others but to ourselves as well.	Low in genuine confidence.
A lack of empathy.		Struggle to feel your opinion is valid, even when you know that it is.
Sometimes present an inflated sense of self-righteousness and morality with very fixed opinions which can't be challenged or debated.	Forgiving of both ourselves and others whilst still able to hold our ground.	Apologize even when you are in the right.
		Find yourself talked over easily.

Mindfulness Meets Emotional Awareness

Mindfulness Meets Emotional Awareness

Chapter 3

Healthy Anger and Aggression

"You are born with a Warrior Spirit, your natural anger.
You can choose to develop your Spiritual Warrior, your healthy
anger,
lined up with your heart."

Source unknown.

We are all no doubt aware of the negative outcomes of aggression and anger, and so for most of us our ability to develop an appreciation of these powerful emotions as valuable can present us with a considerable challenge. Every day we have only to pick up a newspaper or listen to the news to hear of acts of violence that demonstrate the destructive power of these emotions.

In truth, every emotion we have has a place in our lives, even those that fall under the uneasy and uncomfortable category, and each has a part to play in our well-being and in our ability to navigate our lives successfully from a position of self-responsibility and self-care.

One of the best ways to broaden our understanding of any of our more challenging emotions is to think about them as pure, raw emotional components, each one essential, valuable and vital to us.

When we find ourselves troubled by a particular emotion, the problem is never the raw emotional component itself. The difficulty lies in our inability to understand why we are feeling this way and what we can do in response to it. And of course, our responses to any of our more challenging emotions will depend upon our ability to recognize and be aware of the nature and the value of that emotion as well as its relationship to the circumstances in which we find ourselves.

We need to know when, where and how, to express an emotion appropriately.

A while ago, I listened to a recording of a talk given by Dr. Christiane Northrup and she asked her audience a question. *(Additional Resources & Links 6* http://www.drnorthrup.com/ *)*

"Which is the most ferocious animal in the jungle?"

The answers were mixed. Some people said a lion, some a tiger, or maybe a bear.

Her reply was very straightforward, she said:

"It's a mother lion! It's a mother tiger! It's a mother bear!"

"It's a mother something!"

She's absolutely right, and I am sure any wildlife cameraman would back this up. If we wish to encounter pure and immediate aggression, we will find this in the ferocious protection of a mother over her young.

Mindfulness Meets Emotional Awareness

If we were to approach a lioness with a litter of cubs, she would respond to us with pure aggression. But we don't view this as unhealthy, bad or negative. In fact, quite the opposite. We understand and we respect her actions.

She is responding with pure, healthy, protective, nurturing, ferocious aggression and even if we mean her no harm we know that it's appropriate for her to feel aggression towards us. She is entitled to feel that way; it is a natural response.

This raw emotional component of healthy, protective, ferocious aggression is vital to our capacity to be fully engaged in any form of protective care, including self-care.

To stand our ground, and to have a voice, we need healthy aggression integrated into our emotional vocabulary in a language that feels assertive, empowering and manageable.

Not only does this emotion inform us and give us information, often in a very immediate way, it is also the core emotional component that fuels assertiveness, motivation, pride and passion. When we believe in something with a passion and we strive for justice, it is this raw healthy emotional component of aggression that fuels our desire to make a difference and fires us into action.

This is an emotion that generates a high level of energy.

It powers us up when needed and at its best, when channeled appropriately, healthy aggression is an emotion of both action and empowerment.

Mindfulness Meets Emotional Awareness

When we are unable to listen to this core emotion and integrate it into our actions with mindful awareness, not only are we missing the vital information that this emotion brings but we are also shut off from the energy that it gives us. There is nothing passive about healthy, vibrant, nurturing, protective compassion and care.

When we act from a place of 'com-passion' we are acting 'with-passion.' We care and our actions demonstrate this!

So why is anger so very challenging to us? Why have so many of us, learned to fear and to suppress an emotion of such vitality?

The origins of this will vary for each of us, but many of our negative perceptions will have been established and reinforced by experiences of aggression used at its worst and at its most destructive. Combined with an inability to recognize how to use this emotion to good effect, our perceptions will have become established within our mind as a solid belief.

Undoubtedly some of us will have had particularly bad experiences of anger and aggression leaving us with such strong negative associations that we are fearful of any form of anger or confrontation. Even a healthy debate can feel like an insurmountable challenge.

In this instance, we end up missing out on the opportunities that come from vibrant discussion and debate where different opinions expand our perceptions and fuel our growth and learning.

Sometimes, if we have tried to find a healthy voice for our anger but were not heard and our feelings not validated, or indeed if we have experienced oppression at the hands of others, even though our actions demonstrated an appropriate and healthy attitude, then the message we will have learned in association with the expression of healthy anger will be one of pointlessness and futility.

There is a direct relationship between both suppression and oppression of healthy anger and an inner state of despair.

For others whilst they may not have experienced anger or aggression badly, they may simply not have had any kind of role model that demonstrated how to integrate and use this emotion helpfully. It is entirely possible to grow up in an environment of such benign passivity that by its absence a clear message is given: *'Any form of anger is completely unacceptable'*

In the last chapter, I drew a diagram that highlighted the kinds of behavior that are typical of guilt and shame from two ends of a spectrum. To use these emotions to good effect, the healthy position needs to be somewhere in the middle, a state of balance where emotions are recognized, valued and acted upon from a position of mindful awareness.

We can use a similar diagram to enable us to identify how we perceive and manage our anger and aggression. Diagram 2 at the end of this chapter highlights some of the challenges faced with two ends of a spectrum in mind.

Mindfulness Meets Emotional Awareness

Suppression and dissociation from these powerful feelings are at one end of a line, with a complete inability to contain our anger and aggression at the other. Ironically enough the outcome of the behavior that we see at both ends of this spectrum will often result in reinforcing the same underlying, ongoing difficulties.

Both create responses from others which compound a lack of entitlement and an inability to feel heard, creating even more frustration and anger!

At one end of the spectrum, when we suppress our anger or direct it inwardly at ourselves we actively stifle any kind of healthy self-expression. Unable to have a voice that creates any impact in our world, our inner sense of personal entitlement and our capacity to be considerate of ourselves and engage in a life of healthy, protective self-care is continually undermined. This fuels self-doubt, reinforces a lack of confidence and has a significant long-term impact on our self-esteem; indeed, certain types of depression are associated with an inability to be in touch with and express any form of appropriate, healthy, self-respecting anger.

At the other end of the spectrum, when our anger is directed outwardly, spilling over in an uncontrolled manner, we also end up sabotaging our opportunity to be heard and responded to.

One of the most common problems that very angry people experience is the fact that no one ever actually hears what they're trying to say, even when they have a valid point. All people experience and see is the excessive anger.

Mindfulness Meets Emotional Awareness

This reinforces an experience of our thoughts, feelings and opinions being neither recognized or validated which compounds any underlying lack of entitlement. The self-respect that is derived from being in charge of ourselves is absent, with self-value and self-esteem continually eroded, which then in turn, leads to further resentment and a desire to shout even louder!

So, whether anger is turned inwardly and suppressed, or spills outwardly in an uncontrolled fashion, in both situations we inevitably end up not being heard, reinforcing any deeply held perceptions that anger is bad and gets us nowhere. Sadly, whatever had caused our anger in the first place remains unheard and therefore unresolved.

When we stifle or suppress our anger and put it to one side, over and over again, it will stack up.

Eventually something will happen. Something relatively small and insignificant will occur and whether we implode, causing ourselves damage and harm, or we explode, inevitably hurting not only others, but ourselves as well, our reaction will be out of proportion to the situation that we find ourselves in. We have reacted with the stored-up anger that belonged to the previous 50 things that we chose to ignore.

At both ends of the spectrum, navigating the world in a way that actively embraces our healthy, protective, nurturing, ferocious capacity to take care of both ourselves and others, is limited.

We end up feeling badly about ourselves, unable to stand up for ourselves effectively and to negotiate healthy compromises and solutions that enable the core development of trust and the kind of underlying feelings of safety and security that stem from a solid sense of healthy inner entitlement.

Another useful aspect of anger to bring into our awareness is that it is almost always caused or generated by another underlying emotion.

If I were to put of all our emotions in a bottle, anger would be at the top. We only have to look at young children to see this in action. They have yet to learn the social niceties of emotionally acceptable behavior and so, as a consequence their different emotional states are readily available to witness.

If a child is embarrassed - they get angry. If a child is fearful, they may lash out - they get angry. If their feelings are hurt by another child - they get angry. If they fall over in the playground, they will get mad at the tarmac for hurting them - they get angry!

Anger is almost always a response to another emotion and in learning to use our anger effectively it pays us to understand this.

In my experience, people who are easily in touch with their anger, perhaps sitting towards the more uncontained end of the spectrum, will often need help to learn to look below the surface to discover what lies beneath.

Mindfulness Meets Emotional Awareness

Others can be completely immersed in the underlying emotion with no connection to the anger that they need to fuel them into taking an action that could result in a solution or healthy negotiation.

What I am describing is not gender specific, we can all experience these different states of being, however in my therapeutic practice I have met proportionally more men who are needing to be encouraged to look more deeply at the feelings beneath their anger, and proportionally more women who are very much in touch with their underlying feelings, often of hurt and sadness, but desperately need to learn to embrace their anger positively in order to develop their qualities of assertiveness. They have yet to discover the lioness within them.

To a very great extent this is a result of historical social conditioning. I have met many deeply sensitive men who have never learned how to identify any individual emotions beyond that of anger and have been brought up to believe that showing their feelings is an unacceptable sign of weakness and many women who have been brought up to believe that assertiveness is both unattractive and undesirable in a woman.

Regardless of our gender, our nationality and our cultural or social upbringing, one of the greatest challenges we face with this core emotional component is how to develop a healthy form of expression that results in assertive and responsible, considered actions, and in this I am no exception to the rule. This has been an area of particular challenge within my own life.

Mindfulness Meets Emotional Awareness

To do this we will need to confidently develop the necessary language skills to enable us to transform anger into assertiveness in ways that will allow us to be heard, while at the same time taking others into account.

Assertiveness at its best is a tool of negotiation. Many a disagreement could be negotiated differently if time were taken on both sides to work out and vocalize clearly what we really think and how we really feel, in order to give a clear representation of our respective viewpoints.

In terms of developing my own communication skills in this area, what I have learned is this:

In any situation of negotiation or conflict, my recognition of my role in the scenario — and therefore recognition of the choices available to me — creates a position of personal empowerment. Choosing to listen and hear the other person's point of view whilst taking an ownership of my own position with a desire to be an active participant in any negotiation keeps me in my own driving seat.

I do not have any control over the actions of others, nor am I responsible for the actions of others. However, I do have control over my own actions, and I am responsible for the choices that I make in response to the actions of others around me.

Ultimately if we are faced with someone who is never going to listen to our point of view or appreciate our differences with respect and with a desire for negotiation, or indeed if we are faced with someone who says the right things but whose actions do not then follow through with what has been agreed, our anger then serves as the underlying motivator in empowering us to say no and if necessary to walk away completely!

Today's invitation is an exercise based on a series of steps that I have found to be particularly effective in channeling this powerful emotion into a valuable experience with a successful outcome.

Mindfulness Meets Emotional Awareness

My invitation for today

Today I wish to invite you to consider anger as a healthy attribute and to develop the skills to integrate this powerful emotion into your daily healthy living.

My thought for today

"I am responsible for my own choices and my own actions."

When put on the spot, in *'the heat of the moment'*, very few people can think on their feet and come away from a situation confident that they have said exactly what they wanted to say in the immediacy of the situation. Most of us will tend to think of what we really wanted to say afterwards, and I am no exception to the rule.

One of my greatest personal learning curves has been not only to develop my understanding of anger as a vital component in my ability to look after myself, to stand up for myself, and to stand up for the things that I believe in, but I have also needed to develop a method and a language that I could use to support this in the context of my immediate everyday life experiences.

A Useful Exercise

Five steps in the ownership of empowerment and personal choice.
"Notice. Pause. Reflect. Take considered action. Re-evaluate."

Mindfulness Meets Emotional Awareness

- **Notice.** In the first instance, the key to this is to develop your awareness of your feelings so that you notice their arrival before they build up in intensity.

This is a skill that we develop over time. The more that we understand ourselves emotionally, the more readily we recognize when any challenging emotions are surfacing, as well as the valuable information that they bring us. When we feel powerful emotions, then whether it is joyous or challenging, something is going on!

- **Pause.** In any situation where you feel angry, learn to press a pause button. I cannot stress this enough: **learn to press a pause button.**

Now I know that this is easier said than done!

An excellent tool to help with this is to develop a 'stock answer'. By this, I mean a rehearsed sentence or phrase that you carry at the tip of your tongue that will help you to pause and put the brakes on in relation to any kind of automatic, re-active responses.

It is important that you find a language that is right for you otherwise it simply won't feel congruent and 'right' with you.

Let me give you some examples.

If you are someone who feels anger quickly and can lash out at others regretting it later, then a useful phrase might be:

Mindfulness Meets Emotional Awareness

"I'm finding myself feeling really wound up so I'm going to take some time out... I'll come back to you when I've thought this through."

If you are someone who struggles to be in touch with your anger or you automatically concede in a discussion, then a useful phrase might be:

"I can't give you an immediate answer, but I'll come back to you when I've thought this through."

This is a valuable exercise and works regardless of which end of the spectrum you may tend to fall into.

Buying time removes you from the pressure of the moment and creates opportunity for reflection and thought. If you are faced with someone who doesn't listen, repeating your phrase will eventually work. It creates a boundary and reinforces your right to leave the situation and take some time to consider your position.

- **Reflect.** Now is the time to listen to yourself and consider what you think and how you feel, as well as considering the perspective of any other parties concerned.

There is real value at this stage to notice any other underlying emotions that may be influencing your perspective.

I find that brainstorming everything I think and feel on to a sheet of paper is a really good way of being able to stand back from the immediacy of the situation.

Mindfulness Meets Emotional Awareness

Sometimes I might then write a letter to clarify what I wish to say. My intention at this stage isn't to send the letter, it simply serves as a tool of reference to support me in working out how best to proceed.

I then go on to edit this information until it contains all of the relevant points that I need to make, the range of potential choices that are available to me and any conclusions and subsequent decisions that I have come to.

- **Take considered action.** Using the information available to you and your awareness of your choices and possible decisions, take action accordingly.

Assertiveness isn't about asserting our opinion over the opinion of another or at the expense of the opinion of another. It is not a competition.

True assertiveness is an ability to own and voice our own opinion within a state of mutual recognition from a base of healthy self-responsibility and healthy self-care. In situations that involve negotiation with others, any reasonable caring person will welcome an opportunity for discussion and potential resolution.

In conversation, a useful tip is to always own your position, always bring the situation back to yourself and speak about the way that you feel rather than pointing the finger at the other person. For example:

"I find myself feeling…" rather than *"You make me feel…"*

"I find myself thinking about… or wondering about…" rather than *"You are this…"* or *"You are that…"*

This kind of ownership of your own thoughts and feelings within a conversation evokes a far less defensive response from the other party. If needed make a list that you can draw on so as not to forget the points that you need to make.

- **Re-evaluate.** Return to step 3 in the process and use this process of reflection to re-evaluate and re-consider.

Did you achieve a successful outcome? If not, what have you learned from the experience? Brainstorm again, listen to your thinking, listen to your feeling. Use this information to inform and to establish your choices at this moment in time.

Steps 3, 4 and 5 are active components in developing considered choices and empowered decision making. Return to them as ongoing skills in your relational toolkit.

For myself I have found them to be a valuable and effective tool in almost any situation. Even when the choices available to me are not necessarily those that I would wish to have, the clarity brought about by this process of mindful emotional awareness creates a pathway of decision making that has proved time and again to support me in finding the most appropriate way forwards.

"It is wise to direct your anger towards problems, not people; to focus your energies on answers, not excuses."

William Arthur Ward (b. 1921), writer

Mindfulness Meets Emotional Awareness

Diagram 2

Anger Supressed & Turned Inwards		Reactive Anger Uncontained & Spilling Out
Anger & Aggression Supressed &Turned in on the Self.	**A Good Relationship with Healthy Anger & Aggression.**	**Reactive Anger & Aggression Uncontained, Spilling over and Directed Outwardly.**
A tendency to blame oneself.	Able to stand our ground and own our own thoughts and opinions without experiencing the opinions of others as a threat.	A tendency to blame others. Low self-esteem that is sometimes hidden by an appearance of confidence and bravado.
Low self-esteem and lacking in confidence and self-belief.		
Self-sabotaging behaviour. Can sometimes lack motivation and experience periods of low level ongoing depression.	Enjoys negotiation and debate and welcomes difference as an opportunity for expansion and learning.	Self-sabotaging behaviour. Fearful of losing an argument, can't and won't back down.
Experience anxiety and fear in the face of confrontation and would rather back down than have an argument.	Demonstrates assertiveness without the need to force own opinions on to others.	Deep internal feelings of isolation and aloneness.
	Can agree to disagree.	A struggle to maintain harmonious relationships, launching from conflict to conflict.
Reliant upon validation from others to feel worthy.	Able to make conscious decisions followed through with considered action.	
Need permission from others to speak.		Angry reactive outbursts to those closest, pushing people away leaving an even greater sense of isolation.
Failure and confrontation can evoke despair.	Ability to change ones mind through adaptation and conscious learning.	

97

Chapter 4

Healthy Disappointment

"The beauty is that through disappointment you can gain clarity."

Conan O'Brien (b. 1963), entertainer.

In terms of potential contribution in our ability to navigate our lives successfully, I personally believe that disappointment is one of the most underestimated emotions that we have.

In the introduction of this book I wrote about the way that our thoughts and our feelings impact on one another.

Disappointment is an absolutely classic emotion in terms of demonstrating how this works and how the healthy collaboration of mindfulness and emotional awareness can create a complete shift in both our understanding and our approach to our emotional experience.

The way in which our mind receives disappointment and responds to this profoundly valuable emotion will influence our decision making in ways that are literally life changing.

Mindfulness Meets Emotional Awareness

Our capacity to understand the 'information' that disappointment brings and whether we perceive it as 'good information' or as 'devastating news' can either support and empower us or undermine us and send us spiraling backwards.

It is an emotion that can work for us… or against us! And this is not a random outcome; it is a question of choice and as such offers us extraordinary opportunity for personal empowerment.

To understand how this powerful emotion can support us let us first understand the two most common ways in which it tends to derail us and send us off course.

Firstly, certain emotions tend to generate certain types of negative thinking patterns and disappointment is an excellent example of this.

When I spoke about healthy fear and anxiety in the first chapter, I referred to a certain type of thinking pattern as **'Repetitive Thought Syndrome.'** These are the kinds of thinking patterns that are triggered or set off by a certain situation or emotion, leading to thoughts and scenarios that we go over again and again in our mind.

Secondly, certain emotions also tend to spark certain other emotions; one emotional state of being will generate a whole stream of other emotions. And in the case of disappointment, these other emotions tend to fall into the **'Uneasy, uncomfortable'** category.

We all have an internal dialogue or 'running commentary' within our minds.

Mindfulness Meets Emotional Awareness

Sadly, for many of us, this internal conversation is not one of support and positivity. In fact, not only are these conversations unsupportive, but on occasions they are frankly undermining and downright destructive and in the case of disappointment this is frequently so. Learning to observe and to listen to these conversations without judgement and where necessary developing our ability to gently challenge any unhelpful and unsupportive avenues of thinking is a valuable life skill.

Fear and anxiety tend to create a pattern of 'What If?' thoughts with the emphasis on an anticipation of external events that that sit beyond our control. In contrast, disappointment tends to take a far more internal line of thinking, usually of an ultra-critical nature!

The 'Repetitive Thought Syndrome' themes associated with disappointment are frequently those of self-persecution with a storyline that reinforces personal failure, self-doubt, a lack of entitlement and an overbearing sense of personal responsibility accompanied by blame, most frequently directed at oneself.

The storyline of disappointment also often involves a comparison between ourselves and others, with ourselves automatically placed in a lower and less favorable position.

These are the kinds of thoughts I am referring to:

I knew it wouldn't work out!
This always happens to me!
What's wrong with me?
It's all my fault!
Everything I try goes wrong!

Mindfulness Meets Emotional Awareness

Why do I bother?

I don't know why tried in the first place, I knew it wouldn't work out!

I'm just one of these people who is destined not to succeed!

I'm no good!

I'm useless!

Everyone else is fine, I'm the one with the problem!

…. And so it goes on.

The most common emotional states that interweave and are compounded by this kind of storyline are a sense of pointlessness and futility, which if left to run wild can result in a state of very deep despair.

Further 'uneasy, uncomfortable' emotions that are sparked from the primary experience of disappointment are sadness, frustration and anger, usually directed inwardly. These in turn generate underlying feelings of anxiety and helplessness that fuel the potential for despair.

The combination of repetitive thoughts alongside bucket-loads of increasingly challenging emotions can initiate a significant downward spiral that ultimately becomes a self-fulfilling prophesy.

If our self-esteem is low and we are filled with negative thoughts and perceptions about ourselves, then when our internal dialogue becomes one of internal slaughter, what little confidence we may have, will rapidly diminish leaving us feeling increasingly incapable, thus reinforcing our primary position of undeservedness and low self-worth.

Mindfulness Meets Emotional Awareness

As a general rule, repetitive thoughts have their origins in our past experiences and they tend to fall into two categories. Some of these thoughts are the verbal memories of things that we were told. Such as:

You're no good!
You're stupid!
You'll never amount to anything!
It's all your fault!

Others are not necessarily verbal messages given to us by others, but more a picture of the conclusions that we came to about ourselves, about others, and about life itself during our formative years.

As little people, we will come to all sorts of conclusions based on our evaluation of our life experiences, however, it is important to recognize that these conclusions will be based on the perspective of the child that we once were, formed from the limited knowledge and resources available to us at whatever age and stage we were at any given time.

(Additional Resources 7. Child Logic. An audio resource from the Psychology of Emotion Series. © Jenny Burgess A-Z of Emotional Health on-line Library, a free on-line resource http://bit.ly/2p49qMp)

When we begin to make some gentle enquiry as to the content and nature of our inner dialogue and our perceptions of ourselves, of others and of life in general, we often find that we are still navigating life from the perspective of the core beliefs that we formed all those years ago.

Mindfulness Meets Emotional Awareness

This means that to a very great extent we will be viewing our current situation through the lens of past experience formed at a time when we were ill-equipped to deal with the challenges that we were facing.

So repetitive thoughts tend to be a reflection of our innermost beliefs born of our history and our past experiences often accompanied by fears and expectations of the same scenarios and situations happening again.

Now let's discover disappointment as a valuable emotion, the bringer of 'good information,' and let's look at ways in which this vital emotion can become our friend and ally in navigating our way through life's challenges.

Whilst a great many people struggle with disappointment, like all of our emotions, it is never the raw emotional component itself that is the problem, it's what we do with it.

Regardless of the way in which we receive and experience disappointment, as a raw emotional component, disappointment is actually giving us information, and it's good information!

Disappointment means that something hasn't gone well, or at the very least it hasn't gone as we would have liked. By letting us know that something isn't okay, it actually presents us with a profound opportunity.

As we have already acknowledged, whenever we see or identify a problem, our very recognition of the problem creates an opportunity to seek a potential solution or resolution.

Mindfulness Meets Emotional Awareness

If we are seeking to become our own 'inner detective,' then disappointment is a valuable diagnostic tool, as well as an invitation to take action.

When I talk to people about disappointment, I like to use the analogy of a journey. When we find ourselves experiencing disappointment it is as though we have reached a T Junction in the road. A point in our journey that requires us to stop, before making a decision as to the direction we need to take.

Disappointment is a signpost that requires us to put the brakes on, to pause and to do a little bit of diagnostic detective work before proceeding.

Now if in experiencing disappointment we launch into 'Repetitive Thought Syndrome' then we are acting on an automatic response system, usually without pausing for reflection or for considered thought.

These kinds of thoughts, memories and perspectives are an old familiar track, a route that is known to us and, while bizarrely safe and familiar, they take us backwards, living life through the same old lens and the same old perspectives, travelling over the same old ground and potentially responding by repeating the same old patterns.

Our history and our past experiences are influencing our perspective, and sadly often contribute in reinforcing our core beliefs, potentially compounding the problem and creating more of the same: a kind of self-fulfilling prophesy.

Alternatively, we can press a pause button, we can stop at the T-Junction and we can listen.

Mindfulness Meets Emotional Awareness

Disappointment sets the scene for enquiry. It asks us to ask questions.

When we feel disappointment, it is a request to listen to ourselves followed by a call to action.

What is disappointment telling us at this moment?
What is happening here?
What is working?
What is not?
What do you want to do now?
What do you *actually need* to do now?
What is in the best interests of all parties?
How would you really like this to be?
Where would you like to go next?
Which route do you wish to take?
What possibilities are open to you?
What decisions and choices can be made right now?
Do you need more time to reflect?

Let me give you some personal examples of how this has worked out in my own life.

A while ago I decided to start dance classes. It is something that I have always wanted to do but have previously lacked the confidence to try. Part of this was a child perception that I wouldn't be good enough which in turn fueled a fear of disappointment, predominantly in myself!

Now I knew I would be nervous and so ahead of time, I gave myself absolute permission not only to have my nervousness, but I also gave myself permission to have the opportunity to give it a try, have a go and potentially, to be disappointed.

Mindfulness Meets Emotional Awareness

Whenever we try out something that we have never done before there is always the potential for disappointment.

The very fact that something is new to us means that we cannot know if it will work out or not. We have never experienced it before, it is an unknown!

I knew that if I didn't get on particularly well that without doubt, I would feel disappointed, however I also knew that this disappointment would be good information. It wouldn't necessarily mean that I am no good or a failure, or even that dance classes were not right for me. It would simply mean that this particular class wasn't right for me and that I would need to try something else and look elsewhere.

Disappointment doesn't mean that we ourselves are 'bad' or lacking, it means that something within the experience wasn't right for us.

When we engage our inner detective with enquiry and curiosity — rather than judgement and blame — we can begin to work out exactly what didn't work for us as well as what did and, on the basis of this evaluation, work out what we can do about it.

Interestingly enough, this perspective was later reinforced with great clarity.

On that first evening, I actually had a wonderful time. The style of teaching placed a particular emphasis on enjoyment as well as learning and so not only did I begin to learn to dance but I also had a lot of fun and so I continued with weekly classes.

Mindfulness Meets Emotional Awareness

Some months later as my confidence was building, I decided to go to some additional classes in another town, however my experience there was very different.

While the teaching was very good it was clear that it was geared for people who wanted to dance more seriously and any mistakes on my part were not well received. There was a far more critical edge to the feedback without the emphasis of fun and enjoyment that I had become accustomed to and I was disappointed, particularly as I had set my heart on attending more than one class each week.

Now this is an interesting example because it highlights why it is so important to listen to our disappointment.

There was nothing 'wrong' with this class and nothing 'wrong' with me! It is simply that we were not right for each other!

In fact, by engaging my inner detective and listening to my disappointment, I discovered more about myself. I am not only looking to learn to dance but I am also looking for a very particular kind of environment and a very particular kind of learning style.

A relaxed atmosphere and enjoyment are equally as important to me as learning to dance. And so, with this in mind I used this information, I looked further afield and found exactly what I was looking for elsewhere.

My disappointment gave me the opportunity to recognize what was right for me and to make a valid and appropriate choice. It enabled me to become more discerning.

Mindfulness Meets Emotional Awareness

So disappointment gives us 'good information.'

Joining a dance class is of course a relatively small and trivial experience; in truth, our disappointment can take on far greater proportions, especially within our close relationships.

The intensity of disappointment within our most intimate relationships can be hard to bear, however if you experience disappointment within any relationship, intimate, friendship or otherwise, I would urge you to listen to this valuable information.

I recall a relationship of my own in which quite early on I experienced some very significant disappointments. Now disappointment within relationships is inevitable; in reality, it is an important part of getting to know one another as real people, hence it presents us with extremely valuable information with an opportunity to develop discernment with appropriate action.

In this instance, the action required was to initiate conversations with my partner to see whether a mutual understanding could be found, and a resolution sought. This is how we discover what makes each other tick, discover our shared values as well as our differences and find out whether or not we can negotiate compromise and whether or not we will be able to make each other happy.

In this relationship, our outlook and core values were so different that even a conversation proved impossible, producing even greater disappointment; **and yet rather than listen to this as good information I persevered.** I had invested a lot of hope in the possibility of this relationship.

Mindfulness Meets Emotional Awareness

Retrospectively I can see that the circumstances within that relationship so clearly highlights my inability at that point in my life to understand the importance and value of listening to myself.

I ignored my feelings and I persevered, experiencing disappointment after disappointment after disappointment. I attempted conversation after conversation, each resulting in further disappointment and yet rather than listen to this information I remained for far too long in what was already proving to be a significantly challenging relationship with someone with whom I had virtually no compatibility.

If we remain in a challenging situation that is detrimental to ourselves or we remain in a challenging relationship beyond a reasonable time in which we have genuinely tried to find ways forwards, then our capacity for self-care is lacking. We are not listening to the truth of our disappointment nor are we looking after ourselves.

Ultimately, by ignoring my true feelings the eventual separation and breakup was far more traumatic for both of us than it would have been had we parted far earlier.

Whether we are talking about an event or a personal relationship, disappointment provides us with valuable information that offers us the opportunity to make informed and appropriate choices. And whether or not we are aware that these choices are available to us will depend on our ability to notice, to listen, to pause, to reflect and to consider, before making a choice and taking action.

Mindfulness Meets Emotional Awareness

Our ability to effectively put on the brakes, and engage in reflection and consideration, will be relative to our ability to feel our disappointment, and to understand it without reacting to it.

Even when repetitive thoughts kick in or further emotions surface in response to disappointment, when our mind can receive disappointment as a diagnostic tool this will enable us to view our experience from a new and different perspective.

Disappointment can become the instigator of a significant turning point. If desired, we can choose a new direction and take alternative action.

With mindful discernment, this kind of informed decision making can completely alter the course of our lives.

Mindfulness Meets Emotional Awareness

My invitation for today

Today I wish like to invite you to listen to disappointment as a valuable signpost.

My thought for today

"Remove judgement and stay in the questions."

Whenever we find ourselves in a situation where we feel disappointed, we have a choice.

Every single day we are presented with new experiences. Some will work out as we had hoped and some won't. The greater the intensity of our disappointment, the more challenging it is to manage the way that we feel.

Disappointment can be used to reinforce old perspectives that we may hold about ourselves, others and about life in general. Sometimes even the anticipation of disappointment can be used in the service of procrastination, stopping us from showing up and having a go regardless of the outcome.

Alternatively, we can develop an appreciation and value of disappointment as the bringer of "good information".

If we try something out and we have a "bad" or "uncomfortable" experience, by shifting our perspective and engaging with our inner detective we can initiate a voyage of discovery that will give us invaluable life-affirming information.

When we develop our ability to pause and to notice, we develop a collaboration of mindfulness and emotional awareness.

When we learn to listen, with curiosity and without judgement, we create the opportunity to ask the right questions and therefore make considered and conscious choices within the immediacy of our daily lives.

A Useful Exercise

Pause for a moment and bring your attention to yourself.

Think of a situation in which you have experienced disappointment. If you are currently in a situation where you are experiencing disappointment, then bring this situation to the forefront of your mind.

Using a piece of paper or your journal, write the story of your disappointment with any perspectives that you may have about the situation.

Write it as you have experienced it. Listen to your thoughts as well as your feelings and try not to edit yourself.

Now ask yourself the following questions:
- What is my perception of disappointment? Is it valuable or a catastrophe?
- Do my thoughts about disappointment tend to be considered and reflective or unconsidered and more reactive?

Mindfulness Meets Emotional Awareness

- Is disappointment triggering repetitive thought syndrome? Are my thoughts a reflection of previous experience? Do my thoughts follow a pattern or a theme? Have I listened to this storyline before?
- Does disappointment generate other powerful emotions?

Take some time to reflect on your answers to these questions.

Interestingly enough, our repetitive thoughts are telling us a story.

They are telling us about the conclusions that we came to, based on our previous experiences. If we choose to listen to these thoughts and observe them without judgement, we will find within them a mirror of the past.

For example, if we have experienced a previous rejection within a relationship, we may have a fear of that happening again and so our repetitive thoughts may be filled will expectations of future relationships ending up the same way.

If we had once tried something out and found ourselves embarrassed or humiliated, then we will fear this happening again.

Faced with disappointment, either real or anticipated, the content of our repetitive thoughts will be colored by the past. The content of these thoughts will also help us to identify any other underlying emotions that are coloring our decision making, such as fear, anxiety or sadness.

Repetitive thought syndrome is inevitably rooted in history and as such it shows us where we need healing.

Mindfulness Meets Emotional Awareness

With compassionate responsiveness and gentle enquiry, repetitive thoughts are a diagnostic tool in themselves. They offer us the information that we need to understand and identify any support we may need in order to resolve any issues from the past and stop them entering our current situation.

Now go back to the story of your disappointment.

Use the following questions as a guide to help you to reframe the situation from the perspective of disappointment bringing you vital information.

- What is my disappointment really telling me?
- What do I really need to hear from this situation?
- Within this situation can I identify what is working for me and what isn't? How do these answers help to inform me?
- In light of these considerations, what choices are currently available to me?
- Do these answers present me with tough decisions that generate further emotions?
- Do these answers present me with tough decisions and if so where can I seek support?
- Are there any actions I need to take immediately, or is further reflection needed?

Removing any judgement or blame of either yourself or others, take time to just gently sit and stay in the questions. The more that you allow your feelings to be heard, the clearer your answers will be.

"If we will be quiet and ready enough, we shall find compensation in every disappointment."

Henry David Thoreau (1817-1862), author

Mindfulness Meets Emotional Awareness

Chapter 5

Despair: The Ultimate Wake Up Call!

"The words emergency and emergence have the same Latin root 'emergere' meaning 'to arise out of'.
So perhaps the emergencies we face will give rise to opportunities for emergence"

Looby Macnamara, permaculture designer, writer, teacher.

My primary aim in writing this book was to offer an understanding of why we have each and every one of our most challenging emotions, why they are healthy and how we can use them as an asset rather than a disability.

Let me state very clearly. There is nothing healthy about despair. And yet in spite of this, despair is an emotion of profound value to us. Its value is in the message it brings.

Put simply if you find yourself in a state of despair, then something is extremely wrong. From an emotional point of view, despair is the biggest wake-up call that we will ever get!

We need to listen!

Mindfulness Meets Emotional Awareness

I would ask anyone who finds themselves experiencing the depths of this powerful state of emotion to give themselves their full attention. Attention with compassion and a desire for enquiry, without any form of judgement, criticism or blame.

When we experience despair, we need to listen and we need to ask why.

Despair is a state of being that results from a kind of emotional meltdown. Its powerful and debilitating effects usually come as a result of an inability to find any kind of satisfactory response to emotionally challenging circumstances. Unable to either process our experiences successfully or to navigate through, or move beyond and away, from the difficulties that we are facing, we experience a profound sense of helplessness, pointlessness and futility.

Sometimes this can be triggered by a one-off event in which we feel, or indeed are, unable to see a way forwards. But more often despair stems from a gradual build-up, an underlying sense of emotional helplessness that develops over time. This can be in response to a series of events and circumstances, but also sometimes from an ongoing lack of being related and responded to in a way that enables us to feel respected and empowered as a unique and valuable individual.

When we find ourselves continually blocked by either events or people this establishes an environment of 'can't do' and 'impossibility' that erodes our internal sense of entitlement to exert personal choice and to implement change.

Ongoing and pervasive 'stuckness' in any area of our lives perpetuates low self-esteem, sabotages confidence and stifles our creative capacity to find and establish hope as a foundational mindset.

This in turn then undermines our core belief and trust that regardless of present circumstances things can and will change for the better.

For some of us despair has its roots in childhood when we were indeed helpless.

If, for whatever reason, the adults responsible for our care were unable to give us the consistency and reliability that we needed to develop a core sense of trust, we will simply lack a solid foundation of emotional durability at times of duress. This can leave us with a predisposition to experience despair in circumstances that others may find less emotionally challenging.

This doesn't necessarily mean that our parents were bad people setting out to limit our horizons and our possibilities. It simply means that they were not aware of the implications of their actions. Indeed, sometimes parents can inadvertently do all the wrong things for all the right reasons!

If this is the case then, as adults in charge of our own life choices, the more that we develop our self-awareness and our ability to listen to and understand our emotions, the greater our opportunity to take charge of our emotional health and address any deeper insecurities that may still be surfacing within our present time.

Mindfulness Meets Emotional Awareness

Helplessness is an inherent and natural part of any normal childhood.

As children, we are reliant upon the adults in our world to provide us with an adequate degree of protection and safety. For those of us who were fortunate enough to have been parented reasonably well, this will be something that we grew up being thankfully unaware of, however sadly there are situations when adults do treat children extremely badly.

Any form of abuse that violates the natural state of helplessness inherent in every child will create some challenging issues associated with trust. This is completely understandable. If your trust has in any way been violated, there would be something seriously wrong you if you had remained unaffected!

The key to recovery and to moving forwards is what you, as an adult, choose to do about it now.

Physical scars will heal relatively quickly but the emotional ones remain, unseen and therefore often unattended to. When I meet anyone who is struggling with despair I immediately wish to look more deeply.

I am curious about their relationships and the way that they relate, not only with others, but more importantly, with themselves.

When we begin to look below the surface with gentle interest and enquiry, we often find that beneath the despair this person has little or no trust, not only in others and in the world in general, but also in themselves. This lack of trust creates an internal disconnect from hope.

There is a direct relationship between trust and our ability to hold hope in challenging circumstances.

Just as powerlessness and empowerment sit at opposite ends of a spectrum, despair and hope sit at opposite ends of the same line. Hope is a vital component in our capacity for imaginative, creative thought and therefore a vital component in our ability to recover and to move beyond a state of despair.

When we are connected to hope, we are open to possibility.

When we see life through the lens of hope we recognize that even if we cannot see an immediate answer to a problem, we can trust that somewhere or somehow, an answer will be forthcoming and that a solution or a way forwards will be found. Regardless of our circumstances we have a fundamental trust and belief that life can and will change for the better.

By contrast, when we are lacking in trust, our perceptions and our expectations will be colored by an underlying and pervasive sense of unease and anxiety.

A difficulty in trusting others and the world in general will ultimately reinforce a lack of trust in ourselves, undermining our sense of entitlement to make healthy choices as well as our ability to successfully see those choices through. This lack of trust creates an internal experience of ourselves that is shrouded in self-doubt, lowering self-belief and eroding self-esteem.

Mindfulness Meets Emotional Awareness

Hand in hand with hope, the building of healthy self-esteem is another vital component in our ability to move beyond a state of despair.

In fact, if we approach despair from a position of prevention rather than cure, our biggest asset is to build a healthy and solid sense of self-esteem.

Healthy self-esteem underpins our emotional resilience which, combined with an ability to listen to our individual emotional states and respond appropriately, supports us in navigating the constant changes and adaptability to circumstance that life demands of us.

Emotional resilience in adulthood doesn't come from having a perfect and happy existence with no ups and downs in life. Our emotional durability and resilience in the face of human life challenges stems from a core of healthy self-esteem built upon a foundation of trust.

So how do we build self-esteem and how do we maintain it?

The key to this lies in respectful, responsive relationship. Both trust and self-esteem are primarily built through our experience of ongoing respectful recognition and validation within relationship.

We are first and foremost relational beings: we learn to relate through being related to and the consistency and reliability of our primary relationships build within us a core foundation of trust.

As children, we are dependent upon the adults around us to respectfully acknowledge and validate us in ways that support and teach us to navigate our lives with a reasonable degree of confidence and durability. This includes validation and management of the full range of emotions that we experience in the face of our everyday developmental life challenges. For example, fear, anxiety, frustration, disappointment, sadness and anger.

Our emotional durability comes from experiencing the full range of our emotions in ways that fuel and enhance our growth and development. We need to be able to successfully navigate the stepping stones of natural developmental growth, without experiencing emotional overload and overwhelm.

This experience of knowing that we'll be okay, even when we don't feel okay right now, creates an internal sense of stability with an underlying innate sense of trust, which in turn colors our perceptions and attitudes towards any problems or challenges we may later face.

When problem-solving becomes a process of healthy evaluation rather than a black and white, success-or-failure scenario we are free to learn and to grow from our mistakes without being left with underlying feelings of inadequacy and a fear of trying something again.

In a nutshell, we need to be able to make mistakes safely, without fear, without blame and without judgement. If we use the analogy of a small toddler learning to walk, we need to be able to have a go, fall over and get back up again and know that we're okay.

Mindfulness Meets Emotional Awareness

In the real experience of our everyday lives, in whatever we are doing, regardless of the outcome, it is healthy to be able to learn from the experience and to feel good about the fact that we even tried. We also need to feel empowered, enabled and entitled to have another go, or to try a different tack, or if needed, to choose not to do it again!

This is how we learn about healthy decision making and healthy choice. When this process goes well, we learn to trust both ourselves and others with an underlying durability in our capacity to navigate life with trust and confidence, regardless of circumstances.

If you know that your self-esteem is genuinely low and you are struggling with despair then I wish to invite you to make a firm commitment to listen to yourself.

The substance of healthy self-esteem is built through the experience of respectful responsiveness. If you are experiencing despair this is a wake-up call that is requesting your attention.

If you are in an unhealthy and unhelpful situation it is high time you listened to this and gave yourself absolute permission to do whatever is needed to move yourself into an alternative state of mind and an alternative space of feeling.

This may mean finding the courage to reach out and speak to someone. Another contributor to despair is isolation.

If we are isolated or alone, a lack of connection and/or relatedness with others will both compound and magnify our despair!

Mindfulness Meets Emotional Awareness

When we develop an appropriate level of responsiveness to any underlying emotional wounds that we may carry including giving ourselves permission to seek help and support where needed then finding emotional resolution becomes possible.

I recommend building a personal package of emotional self-care that will in itself, create a foundation of ongoing emotional and mental wellbeing. Where needed it will also serve to underpin any process of recovery and resolution from any deep seated emotional scars.

To recover from despair, we will need to re-establish an inner sense of personal safety and from that position, an awareness of any choices that are available to us.

To reconnect with hope, we will need to know that change is possible. To create any form of change we first need to listen and validate the fact that there is a problem.

When we become witness to ourselves with kindness and respect, we can gradually build enough self-worth to emerge from a space of emotional crisis to a space of inner courage where we can re-engage with hope and embrace an empowered state of living, with an awareness of both choice and possibility.

As adults, we can choose to make this commitment to ourselves.

Mindfulness Meets Emotional Awareness

My invitation for today

Today I wish to invite you to create a personal package of self-care that will maintain and increase a healthy state of self-worth and self-esteem.

My thought for today

"Prevention is Better than Cure."

You might be surprised at the number of people who struggle with low self-esteem. Regardless of appearances it is astonishingly common.

A Useful Exercise

There are certain identifying factors or 'trade marks' within people who have low self-esteem that are consistently present and sadly often contribute to maintaining and perpetuating the problem of low self-esteem rather than addressing it.

However, we know that whenever we see and identify a problem it offers us an opportunity. Our awareness offers us a choice.

Using the examples below I would invite you to identify any of these 'trade marks' that might be present for you. Then using the thoughts and suggestions below each one, create a list of things that you might say or do differently.
Having completed your list, create a daily timetable that ensures that you implement these suggestions every day, with consistency and reliability.

Mindfulness Meets Emotional Awareness

We learn through repetition. A toddler doesn't just get up and walk, they learn over time. We don't suddenly pick up a pen and write... we learn over time. The same principle applies to building self-esteem.

It is helpful to develop a package of emotional responsiveness with yourself, and to consistently timetable it into our daily routines.

People with low self-esteem are particularly sensitive to the opinions of others, often becoming skilled 'people pleasers' but at the expense of themselves. They often find themselves saying Yes when they know that they should say No.

When we say Yes to something knowing deep down that we should have said No, we are involved in undermining our own well-being. In essence, we are disregarding or indeed allowing someone else to disregard our own boundaries.

If our primary needs are continually treated with disregard and a lack of respect this will take its toll. However, when we ourselves are actively involved in this process this will both create and perpetuate an erosion of our own internal sense of safety and entitlement. After all, who can we rely on to offer us protection and validation, if we cannot even treat ourselves with this most basic respect?

Mindfulness Meets Emotional Awareness

To attend to this and to re-establish an inner sense of safety we will need to cultivate our ability to establish and maintain our own healthy boundaries. This will in turn establish our trust in our own ability to treat ourselves with courtesy, respect and consideration.

Practice saying No and see what this feels like.

Very often our expectations of being received badly are unfounded, and stem more from a historic fear than our present circumstances.

If you do find saying a healthy No is met with a disrespectful or demanding attitude, however hurtful and disappointing this is, in truth this is actually rather good information! It will tell you a great deal about the person you are dealing with!

You may wish to return to the chapters about healthy disappointment and healthy anger to help to consolidate a way forwards that allows you to listen to these important emotions and use them in developing healthy discernment within your relationships.

Discernment is an extraordinary skill and one that many of us lack in negotiating our choices, particularly within relationships.

In essence, the skill of discernment is simply a process of evaluation and assessment without judgement or blame combined with a sense of solid entitlement.

Mindfulness Meets Emotional Awareness

People with low self-esteem are dreadfully critical of themselves and have a continual flow of an internal critical dialogue.

I would ask you to consider slowing down any internal conversation or dialogue that contains judgement and criticism, and to redefine your expectations of success and failure.

Everything that we do and every choice that we make, may or may not work out! We can never know until we get there!

Cultivate your attitude to all areas of your life as a learning curve and an experiment in discovering what is right for you and what is not.

If we sit in judgement of ourselves as being a good or a bad person, worthy or unworthy, deserving or undeserving, based entirely upon the success of the failure of our choices and actions we will undermine our own confidence and perpetuate low self-esteem whenever something doesn't quite work out.

When we view every experience as an opportunity for discovery which will lead in turn to further choices this is a far more empowering position to place ourselves in. When we remove the judgement, the wrongs and the rights, the internal slaughter… we can transform our inner critic into an internal critique.

Mindfulness Meets Emotional Awareness

We are now in a position to evaluate any of our choices, not in black-and-white terms of success being the way that we thought it would be or had hoped that it would be. Rather that every experience is a success regardless of the outcome and we have an opportunity for re-evaluation and reconsideration and therefore for opportunity for further choice.

Timetable an evaluation period into your day, at least once a week and develop an attitude of personal kindness during your periods of reflection.

Remind yourself that life is a learning curve, and as long as we choose to go with it and to continue learning, both success and failure bring valuable information that supports us in honing our life skills.

Cultivating this perspective means that every choice we make and every action we take creates further opportunities with the potential to learn and to grow.

People with low self-esteem have a tendency to feel guilty even when they have done nothing wrong and can easily take responsibility for the mistakes or problems of others and often over-compensate in trying to put things right.

As we have already understood in a previous chapter, guilt is an important and valuable emotion. Without it we simply wouldn't have a conscience, we wouldn't care!

However, using guilt as an asset in developing self-responsibility and personal integrity is completely different to being overloaded and burdened by guilt when it isn't ours to carry.

Mindfulness Meets Emotional Awareness

Learning that we are not responsible for the choices and actions of others can be a big challenge, particularly if this is a role that we were given at an early age. For someone with low self-esteem being a 'fixer' comes naturally.

It is wonderful to be a caring person and to be a giver, however when we carry more than our fair share of the load, ironically enough, we are actually creating an environment of deprivation for the other person.

Not only do we take away their entitlement to make their own mistakes and grow from their experiences, but when we continually over-give, we create an environment in which we ourselves are unavailable to receive. In doing so we actually block the opportunity for others to give to us and so are active participants in creating relationships of imbalance and inequality.

Over-giving inevitably stems from an underlying issue of some sort and however well-intentioned will inevitably fuel a dynamic that supports some aspect of inequality.

Relationships of balance and equality require a mutuality of giving and receiving.

Practice receiving from others, including their thanks and appreciation and make space in your timetable to foster and validate this life skill.

Mindfulness Meets Emotional Awareness

People with low self-esteem are reliant upon validation from others to feel any sense of self-worth and even when they receive praise, they never fully believe it. They never celebrate their own achievements and regardless of how well they do never feel as though their contribution is good enough.

Self-esteem is built on a foundation of respectful validation. If this was lacking during our formative years then as adults we may find ourselves continually seeking validation from others, unwittingly searching for what was missing in our early lives. This can create a particularly heightened sensitivity to the opinions and moods of others, leaving us vulnerable within relationships across the board.

As long as we are dependent on others for affirmation and validation, we are effectively putting the responsibility for our happiness and personal wellbeing in someone else's hands. In doing so we give away our entitlement for choice and as such, disempower ourselves. In addition to this we are also placing a considerable burden on the other person!

To attend to this, we will need give ourselves absolute permission to develop our ability to acknowledge and validate ourselves. And let's face it, if we asked ten different people what they thought we should do in a particular situation, it is highly likely we will get ten different answers.

In your timetable give yourself regular feedback and evaluation within a defined space of reflection. And remember… **Critique not critic!**

Mindfulness Meets Emotional Awareness

I have regular 'site meetings' with myself where I take time to consider where I am at, what I am happy with, what I might like to change and if so, how I might approach something differently.

This supports me in supporting my own learning and enables me to establish my choices for the following day, the following week and even the following months. It can also help me to define any goals that I may wish to have for the longer term future.

Validate **ANY and ALL** of your achievements, however big and however small. We all know how little problems unattended can build up into a Mount Everest-sized pile of difficulty.

The same principle works in reverse. When we validate our small achievements, and give ourselves continual recognition, then over time this will stack up!

And now finally, I wish to invite you to develop a personal statement or affirmation.

This statement will change from time to time depending on what is uppermost in your life at any given moment. You may also need more than one depending on the specific issues that you are reflecting on.

The purpose of these statements is to give you a tool that becomes a kind of pause button. A statement that stops you in the moment and enables you to cut through any repetitive thinking/feeling/behaving and put the brakes on.

Mindfulness Meets Emotional Awareness

A statement that reinforces and reminds you of your commitment to yourself.

A statement that stops the inner criticism.

A statement that enables you to stand back and be witness to your journey with kindness and a desire to support your growth.

This statement needs to be personal and relevant to you and your current circumstances – and it needs to ring true.

A statement or affirmation that is wonderfully positive but somewhat unrealistic won't carry weight. When we know that something just isn't real, no amount of repetition will make it believable.

Here are some examples:

For many years, I really used to struggle to say No. As a consequence, I found myself overstretched, overburdened and with virtually no real time for myself. My statement or affirmation at this time was about giving myself permission to say No.

"Even though I struggle to say No, I am committed to learning this skill. By prioritizing myself I will ultimately have more to Give others."

I was also fearful of the way that people would see me if I didn't 'get it right for them'. This one didn't just put the brakes on, it would make me smile at the absurdity of my belief that somehow, I should make everyone happy.

Mindfulness Meets Emotional Awareness

"Even though I worry about upsetting people I know that I can never make everyone happy. After all, everyone's a lot of people!"

I worked for a while with someone who had lost all trust in people. Given her experiences I am not surprised, however her perspective about everyone being bad was keeping absolutely everyone at a distance, both good and bad alike. She needed help with this.

"I recognize that some people in the world behave badly but this is not everyone! I am absolutely committed to developing healthy discernment. I support my right to choose who I welcome into my life."

Take some time to develop a statement that is right for you and relevant to your circumstances.

Having developed this statement remind yourself of it frequently. It is easier to recall something in a wobbly moment if we have practiced and rehearsed at a time that is more stress free.

"Hope is the magic carpet that transports us from the present moment into the realm of infinite possibilities"

H. Jackson Brown, Jr. (b. 1940), American author

Mindfulness Meets Emotional Awareness

Chapter 6

Healthy Sadness

"Suffering in its original sense, meant undergoing."

Ralph Blum (b. 1932), author of *The Book of Runes.*

How do we develop and grow into healthy autonomous adults, with our own individual thoughts, opinions and values?

What is it that creates our core sense of self and our identity?

What underpins our ability to build strong, solid, healthy, significant and lasting relationships that enrich our lives and create thriving families and thriving communities?

Finding meaning and purpose in life, working out what matters to us, establishing our core inner values, working out who we want to be and learning to navigate our world in ways that enable us to become the very best that we can be, is not something that simply takes place within our mind using a process of logical thought.

We discover meaning, our likes and our dislikes, our strivings and our passions through the way that we feel.

Mindfulness Meets Emotional Awareness

Every emotion we have contributes in some way to the building of our individuality. The way that we feel shapes our thoughts, our perceptions and our opinions.

Sadness is an emotion that makes a significant contribution in both the development of our individual personalities as well as in our capacity to navigate life in ways that result in us evolving and growing from our life experiences.

Anyone who has experienced a challenging or traumatic situation will know that the scars that inevitably remain are the emotional ones. Unseen and often unacknowledged, when left unattended their influence remains powerful and can result in no end of ongoing problems.

When we talk about people carrying 'baggage' we are talking about their inability to have successfully moved beyond an experience from their past. In some way, they are still attached or tied to the experience. They haven't been able to grow beyond it.

Let me be clear that working through something does not mean forgetting. Working through something means that we have been able to process the memory of an experience so that it no longer emotionally haunts us or continues to dictate our responses in the present time.

A crucial part of this 'working through process' involves sadness and an ability to grieve. When I speak about grieving I am not only referring to the grieving process that we associate with bereavement.

Grieving is a vital part of everyday life.

Mindfulness Meets Emotional Awareness

Life is an ongoing process of growth and therefore of change and every change will involve some kind of loss, the loss of how something was.

When we process our experiences, and as we reflect and make sense of our experiences, they become integrated into our bank of knowledge. This is wisdom! And it is through this process of integration that we successfully navigate the stepping stones and learning curves of natural development and growth.

In my experience when we carry 'emotional baggage' it is frequently an indication of an inability to grieve for something that has taken place. An inability to 'feel' our sadness about what has happened and an inability to understand the validity of our sadness and to use it to good effect in the laying of the past to rest.

When we let go of something, a person, a chapter of life, a job, a situation, a home… when we move on, whether it is by personal choice or by circumstance, we are involved in the process of loss. And this will initiate the process of mourning.

Even when we seek a desired change, and are naturally moving forwards as planned, there is often an element of sadness involved in processing the emotional experience of this transition.

(Additional Resources 8. The Sadness of Moving Forwards. An audio resource from the Psychology of Emotion Series. © Jenny Burgess A-Z of Emotional Health on-line Library, a free on-line resource http://bit.ly/2vEgMtJ)

Mindfulness Meets Emotional Awareness

Transitions occur at numerous different stages of life. Each time we move forwards, embracing the next chapter of our life, we are also letting go of a previous chapter.

Now this chapter may have been a wonderful and fulfilling period in our lives, and we may well be looking forward to the next chapter with joyful anticipation, but regardless of our positive expectations, it is absolutely natural to experience an edge of sadness as we let go of a joyful period of time in our lives.

Likewise, if we move into a new chapter of life, from a place that wasn't okay, desiring change above all else, it is still natural for us to experience sadness as we move forwards. When we let go of a difficult chapter of life, we will need to grieve for time lost, for time that was not enjoyed to its fullest.

Grieving for time lost is particularly common for anyone whose childhood was difficult or challenging. In these kinds of circumstances, when we begin to lay the past to rest and really move forwards successfully, we will need to grieve for the childhood that we didn't have. As we process and put down any history that we have been carrying, as we work through these difficult past experiences, sadness will naturally emerge.

We will need to grieve for the absence of those things were missing for us, for the absence of a childhood full of love and protection and nurture.

So, sadness is an appropriate emotion during any important transition.

Mindfulness Meets Emotional Awareness

In truth, there are many occasions when we can feel profoundly sad and appropriately so, however without the understanding of '*why*', these powerful feelings can be interpreted as a 'problem'.

When there isn't something immediately obvious that we can easily identify, or when we feel that our sadness is out of proportion to the event, or we believe that we should have let it go or moved on from it some time ago, we may struggle to give ourselves permission to acknowledge the validity and importance of our feelings.

However, if we stifle or deny these feelings then we will be unable to identify or connect to the root cause of them and this will inhibit our capacity to successfully attend to ourselves and to move through and beyond this experience.

In bereavement, when we lose someone that we love, we expect to feel sad, and as such in these circumstances our feelings are considered acceptable and therefore okay. Because we have an appreciation of sadness being a valid emotion during the process of loss and bereavement and because we understand this, our sadness feels valid. It is as though we are 'allowed' to feel this way.

I do however wish to state that in my experience, the socially acceptable timescales afforded us within western culture often fall a long way short of the time needed to successfully process the loss of a significant person!

This is also the case when a significant relationship ends. The process of losing someone that we love who is still around, maybe even seeing someone else, is huge, and time is needed to fully process this experience.

Mindfulness Meets Emotional Awareness

An important part of this 'working through process' is one of emotional release. The sadness and the tears that accompany this powerful emotional state actually help us to release mental and physical stress and tension.

I think we all know in principle that bottling up our feelings is unhelpful, and yet so many of us still carry an inherited belief system that leaves us unable to show our emotions and to reach out for support when we need it.

I suppose that one of the challenges we face is in recognizing that our sadness is relevant and valid, even when the underlying cause of our feelings may not be immediately obvious. Sometimes when we feel sad but don't understand why we feel this way, we can become fearful and mistrusting of our feelings and worried about ourselves in ways that can add to the emotional burden.

I have come across a significant number of people who struggle with an underlying sense of pervasive sadness and melancholy that fluctuates in intensity but never quite seems to leave them.

As we begin to gently explore their underlying feelings, we discover that they are involved in a massive multi-layered process of mourning, not only for previous losses and events of the past but for the ongoing implications and losses that they have experienced subsequently in many areas of their lives, often over many, many years.

Mindfulness Meets Emotional Awareness

To help them to move on, we need to recognize, acknowledge and validate the importance and relevance of their feelings and support them through this vital experience of transformation through grieving.

The acceptance and validation of our emotions with compassion and understanding, combined with the release of tension and stress plays a huge part in any form of emotional recovery.

As they begin to emerge from within this process, the understanding gained through their sadness confirms and consolidates their deeper, inner feelings and values.

The substance of our values and the things that matter to us do not only come from discovering happiness and the aspects and elements of life that bring us joy. It is also through our experience of sadness that we discover meaning.

Even in experiences of profound adversity, it is often our greatest challenges that ultimately strengthen our core inner values making us the person that we have become. Despite adversity we have still managed to find a gain, often with a considerably greater integrity and awareness.

Author and psychiatrist Victor Frankl, a survivor of the holocaust, said:

"Suffering ceases to be suffering when it finds a meaning."

This doesn't actually mean that we cease to suffer or that we no longer experience our challenging emotions.

Mindfulness Meets Emotional Awareness

It means that we acknowledge and validate the meaning of our feelings. We allow ourselves to experience these emotions in a manner that deepens our understanding whilst strengthening our opinions, our value systems and our sense of personal identity.

Some of the most successful and well-balanced human beings that I have ever met have risen from the ashes of extremely challenging and abusive childhoods.

Despite everything that has happened to them, through processing their experiences and in successfully 'working through' their history, particularly the emotional residue of those experiences, they develop a deep appreciation of who they have become, in spite of and regardless of their past.

The strength of their convictions and their passion to live differently has stemmed from adversity.

There is no question that the events of their past should never have taken place. There are no circumstances in which any form of violation or abuse should ever be condoned or supported, but I can tell you that it is an extraordinary and powerful moment when someone can appreciate themselves despite their history and celebrate the core values that they hold so deeply. Core values which have fueled their inner strength and resolve, their sense of justice and their passion to create a better world!

Healthy sadness has an integral role to play in our development as individual human beings.

Mindfulness Meets Emotional Awareness

It is one of the key emotions that helps us to develop our opinions and value systems, and therefore plays an integral role in the development of our personality.

Sadness enables us to navigate transition successfully and to grow from the experience in ways that puts the past behind us whilst integrating our memories and experiences into our bank of knowledge. Indeed, sadness is integral to our capacity to develop appreciation.

Without the backdrop of sadness, we would have no capacity to differentiate between an experience of positive or negative significance. Or as is frequently the case, a combination of both, life is rarely completely black and white.

Healthy sadness also often accompanies other emotional states and supports us in our capacity to process those emotions in ways that enable us to evolve and to grow. We can see how this works if we think about sadness in connection with some of the other challenging emotions that we have already explored in previous chapters.

Disappointment is often accompanied by sadness and this is appropriate. We know that disappointment is an emotional state that is full of information: it is asking us questions. It is the accompanying sadness that allows us to grieve or mourn for whatever wasn't working.

As we listen to our sadness and appreciate its importance and relevance to our situation, we can make informed and appropriate choices whilst releasing any emotional tension or residue that is left within us.

Mindfulness Meets Emotional Awareness

Our process of grieving supports us in letting go of whatever wasn't working for us, clearing the way to move forwards to new opportunities and new possibilities.

Likewise, with anger, the accompanying sadness will support us in discovering the underlying source of these feelings. Anger is a reactive emotion, often triggered by a deeper feeling within us, very often a sadness. Something has caused us to feel angry. Perhaps we are hurting or afraid.

The recognition of our accompanying sadness can help us to slow down and move from a space of *'reaction'* to a space of *'reflection'*, pausing our anger and opening a doorway for a deeper exploration centered in compassion.

Sadness is also the foundation stone of compassion. When we feel compassion, primarily we feel sad.

Compassion is a combination of sadness, with a healthy dose of nurturing protective ferocity thrown in. Their union gives birth to our desire for change and to make a difference. *'Compassion'* literally means *'with-passion'*.

Our sadness brings our attention to something that isn't okay. Our anger, our passion, fuels our sense of justice and brings motivation and impetus to our desire to change something, to find a solution and to find ways of doing things differently.

So let us understand and welcome any sadness that arrives at any time in our lives.

Mindfulness Meets Emotional Awareness

Whether we are conscious of its origins or not, the presence of sadness graces us with an opportunity to identify challenges both past and present, to process and to let go of the past, to release our emotions and to navigate healthy, creative change, transition and growth.

Mindfulness Meets Emotional Awareness

My invitation for today

Today I wish to invite you to challenge any negative perceptions and beliefs about sadness that may be blocking you from moving forwards. I would also like to invite you to celebrate and to value this powerful emotion.

My thought for today

"The key to overcoming sadness is responsiveness."

Learning to grieve and our expectations of happiness.

We know that if we are to successfully overcome and 'work through' any form of emotional challenge, we will need to recognize, acknowledge and validate the way that we feel. It is unhelpful to bottle up our feelings and to ignore them.

In the classic Pixar film *Inside Out*, the story follows Riley, a little girl who is struggling with circumstances in her life that bring up the full range of her challenging emotions. This is a wonderful film that beautifully demonstrates the value and importance of sadness.

There is a moment in the film, when 'Joy' tries to stop Riley from feeling 'Sadness', with catastrophic consequences.

Mindfulness Meets Emotional Awareness

Riley's inability to feel her sadness combined with her mother's need for her to remain happy cause her to emotionally shut down. Until she became able to *'take ownership'* of her sadness and speak openly about it, she was unable to grieve for a chapter of life that had changed.

Her feelings needed acknowledgement and validation in order to identify her current challenges and to find the support that she needed to move forwards and successfully make the transition to confidently embrace a new set of life circumstances.

This film beautifully illustrates the impact of an inability to recognize and validate sadness within what would be considered 'everyday normal circumstances', with busy parents who are facing their own life challenges, are stressed themselves, and are therefore unable to attend to their daughter's feelings.

As the story progresses and Riley's sadness is acknowledged, we visibly see her sadness becoming integrated into memory, bringing both meaning and resolution into her life.

A Useful Exercise

In today's exercise, I wish to challenge any negative perceptions or beliefs that you may carry about sadness that may be getting in the way or blocking you from using this vital emotion to support you as you journey through life.

Some of you will be familiar with the term 'limiting beliefs'.

A limiting belief is a perception that we hold within our mind that blocks us in some way, limiting our belief in ourselves and therefore limiting the scope of our horizons.

Some of these beliefs will have come from the social and cultural expectations that surround us, many of which we still see and hear being reinforced such as, 'showing emotion is a sign of weakness!' or 'boys don't cry!' Other beliefs will be deeply personal and often have their origins in our childhood.

These kinds of personal beliefs come in all different shapes and sizes and are influenced and colored by different emotions. We hear aspects of these beliefs in the content of the internal dialogue of 'Repetitive Thought Syndrome' as discussed in previous chapters.

Almost all of us, either consciously or unconsciously, will hold some negative perceptions or beliefs about sadness.

Interestingly those that are related specifically to sadness are often held in mind in ways that are connected with expectations of happiness.

Here are some examples:

I don't deserve to be happy!
I make everyone unhappy!
If mum and dad are unhappy it must be my fault!
I need to show that I'm happy all the time!
If I'm not happy, there must be something wrong with me!
I must keep everyone happy!

These kinds of beliefs both deny sadness whilst simultaneously creating more of it!

Mindfulness Meets Emotional Awareness

Most of us will have grown up in a world where at some time or another our families will have faced some sort of challenge, not unlike Riley. This is the stuff of normal, real, everyday life!

Our understanding of the importance and the need for emotional literacy is a relatively recent development and so for most of us, the families in to which we were born will not necessarily have had an awareness of how to manage their own emotions at times of stress — let alone ours as well — and this will have left its mark.

People who struggle with low self-esteem often have a veritable library of limiting beliefs about themselves, which they visit on a reliably regular basis, reinforcing internal self-doubt and self-criticism, continually lowering their fundamental belief in themselves, their gifts, and their abilities.

A tangle of challenging emotions wrapped up in repetitive thinking patterns that are loaded with self-criticism, can become a self-fulfilling prophecy in a cycle of living that recreates and compounds these deeply held perceptions, perpetuating low self-esteem and a lack of confidence.

Likewise, if we have experienced any form of violence or abuse during childhood this can leave us with a huge emotional legacy loaded with beliefs and expectations. The betrayal of trust by grown-ups who should have been there to protect, but actively violated their position of trust, often knowingly and deliberately feeding a child's self-doubt in order to maintain their silence, will inevitably have generated a multitude of beliefs that will need to be gently challenged with care and compassion.

Mindfulness Meets Emotional Awareness

If this applies to you please never be afraid to find help and support. The legacy of childhood abuse may be huge but if any aspect of our childhood has been violated, then all the more reason to ensure that our adulthood is enjoyed in its fullest capacity!

Take a piece of paper, more than one if necessary, and draw a line down the middle.

On the left-hand side of the page, list any negative cultural and social perceptions that you have experienced about sadness.

On the right-hand side of the page, list any negative personal beliefs that you have developed in relation to yourself and your own experiences of sadness. Include any beliefs, expectations or obligations about happiness.

Next, making some space where you will not be disturbed, sit down with your list and quiet your mind.

Imagine a child sitting in front of you. The beliefs on the page in front of you belong to them.

This child is struggling to 'take ownership' of his/her sadness and speak about it.

His/her feelings need acknowledgement and validation in order to identify any current challenges and to find the right support to move forwards.

Mindfulness Meets Emotional Awareness

The kind of support that would develop inner strength, inner resolve and emotional durability, the key components of healthy self-esteem.

Go through each of the beliefs and expectations one at a time. Imagine what you would say to the child sitting in front of you.

If they grew up in a world where showing feelings was considered a weakness, what examples might you give them to help them to see this differently?

What kind of language would you use to gently challenge his or her perceptions in ways that would allow them to understand the validity of their feelings?

What kind of language might you use to offer reassurance and help them to explore their feelings further without judgement or blame?

If they believe that they have to keep 'everyone' happy, then how might you encourage them to work through this overwhelming burden! After all, 'everyone' is a lot of people!

How would you support them in generating hope with a belief in themselves and a belief in their future?

How would you let them know that they don't need to have all the right answers right now and that the best solutions are found over time!

How will you support them in experiencing and releasing the sadness that will inevitably be present from living in such a constricted world?

153

Mindfulness Meets Emotional Awareness

©Jenny Florence/Burgess A-Z of Emotional Health Ltd 2016 All rights reserved.

Our emotional health isn't about being happy all of the time, and happiness doesn't come from blocking out our sadness.

The key to processing our healthy sadness lies in responsiveness.

We don't have to find solutions and answers immediately. We do however need to learn to listen to ourselves and be appropriately responsive with care, compassion and kindness: this enables us to be resilient and to be okay regardless of what's going on in our world.

"The most beautiful people we have known are those who have known defeat, known suffering, known struggle, known loss, and have found their way out of those depths."

Elisabeth Kubler-Ross (1926-2004), Swiss-American psychiatrist

Mindfulness Meets Emotional Awareness

Chapter 7

Healthy Envy and Jealousy

Envy comes from people's ignorance of, or lack of belief in, their own gifts.

Jean Vanier (b. 1928), author, traveler, humanitarian and peacemaker

When we feel envy, we see in others something more than we ourselves are. We see something that we ourselves have yet to be or to achieve, or indeed some aspect of our own aspirations that we have been unable to step up and become.

When we feel jealousy, we see that others 'have' something; an object, material wealth or a person that we ourselves would like, but do not have.

If we consider that a yearning or a desire can form the foundation of a dream and become the beginning of a creative endeavor from which an entire life's journey can be shaped, then in essence, both envy and jealousy are emotions that contain seeds of potential and therefore present us with doorways of opportunity.

At their best, both envy and jealousy can form the basis of one of the most inspirational and empowering emotional states of being, a launchpad from which we are inspired to achieve and to become more than we currently are.

At their worst, powerful feelings of envy and jealousy that derive from seeing in others that which we are not and that which we do not have, can generate a state of mind which left unfettered results in some of the most poisonous acts of human destructiveness.

In a flourishing environment where individual desires are respected and our different gifts nurtured and valued equally, envy and jealousy can transform into a healthy competitiveness with a camaraderie in which we feel inspired and supported in becoming the best that we can be with a healthy ownership of both our fullest potential alongside our realistic limitations.

This kind of healthy competitiveness generates inspiration and motivation, derived from a core demonstration of value and worth of both ourselves, and of others, resulting in the recognition of our own strivings, and a pride and an enjoyment in both our own achievements as well as in the achievements of others.

This healthy validation and celebration sits at the core of healthy teamwork where individuality sits alongside collaboration with an honest recognition and appreciation of the value of each and every person's contribution to the whole.

When we can celebrate and literally 'en-joy' the achievements of others and recognize any underlying feelings of envy and jealousy as an opportunity to broaden our own horizons, this is without doubt a mark of maturity within our own evolutionary growth.

Mindfulness Meets Emotional Awareness

Cherishing our own choices based on the reality of what we really want for ourselves without any need to take an ownership or a piece of anyone else's achievements is a mark of becoming a healthy, individual, autonomous human being.

When envy and jealousy are acted out in a destructive manner, there is no capacity to enjoy the achievements of others. Interestingly enough, a by-product of these powerful emotions unleashed destructively is that there is also no genuine inner capacity to enjoy or to celebrate oneself either.

At the root of envy and jealousy in its most destructive form, we will inevitably find some kind of inner wound. Somewhere along the line our needs have not been met, resulting in an inner emptiness and a lack of a sense of being worthy oneself. This is then compensated for or managed, by blocking opportunities for others or indeed sabotaging their success, sometimes overtly but more often in a manner that is underhanded or 'below the belt'.

The erosion of the well-being of others, either overtly or covertly, will also erode our own inner sense of well-being. There is no self-respect or genuine honor in sabotaging the worth of others.

Destructive behaviors formed on the basis of envy and jealousy perpetuate a cycle of low self-esteem and become a self-fulfilling prophecy where deliberate intention to sabotage others will inevitably also become a form of inner personal self-sabotage.

In the first book that I ever wrote, "Emotional Health, the Voice of our Soul", I likened the health and well-being of our self-esteem to the health and well-being of the soul.

Mindfulness Meets Emotional Awareness

When we hurt others and deliberately set out to cause them problems or to limit their horizons, regardless of the way that we justify this to ourselves, or indeed present a version of events to the world that denies our part in the scenario, when a declaration of innocence is untrue it will erode any capacity for genuine self-respect.

Ultimately, regardless of the way that we present ourselves outwardly, we are the ones that will have to live with the knowledge of our actions.

In a nutshell, when we behave badly, regardless of whether or not we are able to get away with it in the eyes of others, ultimately, we are accountable to ourselves and the result of treating others badly will erode and damage our own internal sense of self-worth and eat away at our inner sense of personal honor and well-being. Our actions are quite literally 'soul-destroying'.

Many years ago, I came across a man who had recently come out of a long-term marriage. He had two sons. As I began to get to know him, I learned that his eldest son was an extremely talented footballer and that he had been 'spotted' and offered the opportunity to attend a specialist football school.

Now I know very little about football but was told that at that time, thirty years ago, that this was the only football school of its kind and that to be offered such a place was a virtually guaranteed opportunity or entrance point to become a professional footballer with a potential pathway to considerable success, fame and wealth. This lad adored his father and would have done anything to please him.

The father's own background was one of tremendous challenge: an upbringing fraught with physical, sexual and verbal abuse and steeped in profound poverty. Very few opportunities had been available to him and so completely understandably, with no support in processing his challenging history to help him to move beyond the legacy of his past, he had little confidence in his own worth or value.

With extremely low self-esteem, he struggled in almost all areas of his life, including financially where he frequently undercharged for his services and yet then resented his customers for their apparent lack of value and appreciation of his hard work.

When his son was offered the place, he congratulated him but then gave him a list of tasks and chores that he would need to achieve before he would allow him to go to the school.

The list was unachievable, an impossibility for any adult, let alone a child!

When the day came for the son to go to the school, his father refused to allow him to go, stating very clearly that it was the child's own fault. His son hadn't achieved the chores that were requested of him and therefore — in the father's own words — *"how could I let him go when he had let us down so badly? It was his own fault. He gave me no choice!"*

Of course, the truth is that the father did have a choice. He could have chosen to cherish his son's talent and opportunities.

Mindfulness Meets Emotional Awareness

His actions demonstrate a classic example of profound and deep envy. This man simply could not bear his son being successful. Rather than enjoying and celebrating his son's achievements, he set about sabotaging his opportunities. And the result was a tragedy for them both.

Their relationship deteriorated and the son, who as a teenager was beginning to help his father in his business, began to feel profound resentment towards him with an underlying envy of other young people around him who he saw as having far more opportunity than he did.

Completely unconsciously, and under very different circumstances the father handed down a legacy of 'I don't deserve and I can't have', repeating a pattern that was in much need of change!

Despite his justification, I am sure that deep down the father did not feel particularly good about himself, his actions ultimately eroding his view of himself as a deserving human being.

At their most destructive, envy and jealousy result in a powerful drive to exert power over another.

The need to exert power over others in ways that hurt, limit and sabotage are frequently driven by envy and jealousy and often the root cause of bullying.

When bullying is overt and obvious, it is easier to tackle. When we clearly see that someone is behaving offensively or directly violating another, the clarity of their actions gives us permission to step up and to say No! The line between wrong and right has already been defined.

Mindfulness Meets Emotional Awareness

Passive or underhanded bullying is far harder to address, not only for the target(s) of the bullying but also for onlookers who know that something isn't right but feel disempowered to intervene.

I am sad to say that I have come across many instances of passive bullying directed at people who are successful, try hard and achieve, or simply go the extra mile.

I lived for a while in a town where within a particular social group, the predominant culture was to take a pride in doing as little as possible whilst subtly undermining anyone who thrived.

Anyone who stood out as being different or successful was noticeably put down, often behind their back with negative information about them presented and discussed in ways that sounded very plausible but was clearly designed to tarnish their success and taint their reputation.

As a result, anyone who did well for themselves seemed obliged to apologize for doing so, either embarrassed at their success or unable to own the outcome of their hard work for fear of being ostracized or for fear of making others feel less worthy about themselves.

Living for any amount of time in an environment of passive sabotage and targeting will leave significant emotional scars that will need a deeper level of understanding to heal.

Mindfulness Meets Emotional Awareness

Whenever I take my mind back to that time in my life I am reminded of one of my favorite quotes by Marianne Williamson — words later used by Nelson Mandela in his 1994 inaugural address:

"Our deepest fear is not that we are inadequate. Our deepest fear is that we are powerful beyond measure.
It is our light, not our darkness that most frightens us. We ask ourselves, Who am I to be brilliant, gorgeous, talented, and fabulous?
Actually, who are you not to be? You are a child of God.
Your playing small does not serve the world. There is nothing enlightened about shrinking so that other people will not feel insecure around you.

We are all meant to shine, as children do. We were born to make manifest the glory of God that is within us.
It is not just in some of us; it is in everyone and as we let our own light shine, we unconsciously give others permission to do the same. As we are liberated from our own fear, our presence automatically liberates others."

I often read this quote to people when they are working through the emotional consequences of living around those who have invested in passively eroding any vision of possibility in their lives and are needing to discover and embrace a greater level of personal empowerment.

True empowerment does not mean exerting power over others. It means exerting power over ourselves!

In contrast with the environment I have just described, just a few weeks ago I had a wonderful conversation with a very dear friend.

Mindfulness Meets Emotional Awareness

Now in his mid-fifties, this is a man who has been extremely successful in his life, including his career. We had agreed to meet to discuss a young apprentice coming through his company.

My friend was saddened by the lack of motivation and the lack of pride that this young person demonstrated in his work and wanted to talk through ways in which he might be able to help.

When my friend, a Yorkshireman from a tough working-class background had left school, he had himself done a rigorous five-year apprenticeship. He lit up as he described the healthy competitiveness in the environments that he had worked and trained in. How he and other apprentices would come in early, striving to achieve more and to be the best… and the gentle banter and ribbing when something wasn't quite as good as it could be.

But he said:

"Not the way that banter is used as a put-down! Not the kind of naming, blaming, shaming game that creates an environment of humiliation where people feel awful, inadequate and hopeless, in fact quite the opposite.

The banter was wrapped in a kindness with a willingness to help, a recognition that it would be possible to overcome and to do better and to achieve a genuine sense of pride in the quality of workmanship.

We didn't laugh <u>at</u> one another we laughed <u>with</u> one another.

Mindfulness Meets Emotional Awareness

We would all come in early to see who could get there first and stay late to finish a piece of work first. There was a healthy, competitive striving to see whose work could be the best and we admired each other's accomplishments and achievements!

Ultimately along with the banter and the joking, each of us was developing and learning about pride. We each began to learn and respect that we all had slightly different aptitudes in different areas and that we would benefit from helping each other.

There was a camaraderie that was both competitive and respectful. It was one of the most supportive environments I have ever known. We learned to do things properly and we took pride in doing so."

I think that it is exactly this attitude that we see in healthy competitive sport, when people aspire to be like the heroes they grew up admiring and aspiring to be like. Wanting to be as good as their predecessors, indeed desiring and dreaming of being even better than that!

Striving to train and to push themselves to be more. Taking a pride in winning. Not at the expense of others, or with the need to put someone else down or to laugh at someone else for being less than themselves, but taking pride and an ownership and a joyous celebration of their personal achievements in ways that inspire others to do the same.

The legacy of an ability to celebrate our own achievements is a core quality of many a gifted teacher.

People who feel fulfilled and good about themselves can impart knowledge and take a pride in the achievements of others as they flourish, knowing that the next generation will in turn take our original performance and with the right support and encouragement, do even better.

What fulfilment means in real terms will of course be different for each of us, and rightly so. What one person desires and aspires to will be completely different from the desires and aspirations of another, however — in the western world at least — we are bombarded by imagery and information at an unbelievable pace and these influences can set certain parameters of expectation.

Sometimes an inability to find personal fulfilment, or to feel that the life we have been living has been purposeful, comes from an inability to find external validation that is congruent with our own values and lifestyle.

In the face of societal pressures and expectations or in the eyes of others, we can be left feeling that our gifts and contributions are in some way inferior to those of others and that we simply haven't made the grade.

In the last couple of years I have come across an increasing number of people who feel as though their lives are not living up to the social expectations of their peer groups as portrayed via Social Media.

A dear friend recently shared a particularly astute quote that referenced the way that social media has created an environment where the sharing of life's highlights can be a very edited and polished view of how a person really lives: the reality being far more mundane.

Mindfulness Meets Emotional Awareness

'Don't compare your backing track with everyone else's show-reel.'

I loved this quote.
This level of external pressure can create a real challenge in terms of each of us working out what is actually right for us as individuals.

Negative perceptions of ourselves causes and maintains an inner lack of worthiness and self-value. I am always minded when I meet people who feel this way about themselves to ask them what has truly made them happy, and to encourage them to value what is important to them, rather than trying to meet any current social trends and perceived requirements or status.

For some people, despite having opportunity, they have not been able to find the confidence to step up into the world and become everything that they might have wanted to be.

On many occasions, I have seen both envy and jealousy of others present in those who for whatever reason have been unable or reluctant to truly invest in themselves. In not allowing themselves the opportunity to have the kind of life they would really have liked, their subsequent resentment turns into envy and jealousy directed at others.

Mindfulness Meets Emotional Awareness

I have also met people who whilst they have a burning desire to have more, usually with an emphasis on material wealth, have no inclination whatsoever to step up and take on the level of responsibility and hard work that would be needed to build, let alone sustain, the kind of lifestyle that they imagine they would like. And yet they openly resent those who have worked extremely hard to be in the more lucrative position that they find themselves in.

In this instance the saying, 'be careful what you wish for' comes to mind.

In truth, we may sometimes imagine we might like the lifestyle that we assume or perceive that someone else has and yet the reality of such a position with the restrictions, exposure and vulnerabilities that come with this kind of lifestyle might be far from what we would really want for ourselves on a daily basis.

We would do well to consider a more real picture with a genuine awareness of the reality of that dream. This level of honesty with ourselves is of real value in managing our underlying feelings and in working out what happiness and contentment may mean to each of us in real terms.

So how do we turn envy and jealousy into inspiration and fulfilment?

In the first instance to use these emotions effectively we will need a degree of self-awareness and an ability to be honest with ourselves.

Envy and jealousy are hard emotions to own, and their presence often initially generates shame, which in turn is a tough one to feel good about.

Mindfulness Meets Emotional Awareness

If shame is a challenging emotion for you please use the chapter about shame and guilt to help in finding some clarity about this emotion.

Secondly, we will need to have a healthy degree of self-esteem.

At a core inner level we will need to feel worthy and deserving with an inner sense of entitlement that, regardless of circumstances, supports a mindset that acknowledges our capacity for free will and for choice, with recognition that consequences occur as a result of our choices.

Thirdly we will need a degree of motivation that enables us to take action.

And lastly, we will need to be 'real' with ourselves.

We will need to be able to reflect without judgement, blame or criticism thus creating an internal state of mindfulness that enables healthy and honest evaluation.

As long as we evaluate personal success in terms of social expectations or we are driven by unrealistic perceptions that disguise the reality of the bigger picture, we deny ourselves the opportunity to discover what fulfilment really means to us and to find our own unique and individual pathway in finding contentment.

My invitation for today

Today I wish to invite you to establish your core inner values and from this foundation create the opportunity to discover purpose and your own unique pathway to fulfilment.

My thought for today

"True empowerment does not mean exerting power over others, it means exerting power over ourselves"

We cannot discover a direction or our own unique pathway to a life of fulfilment without first working out what actually matters to us.

Our differences mean that each of us has the potential to find self-fulfillment and purpose in whatever direction is right for us as individuals with our unique gifts and potential for contribution.

At the core of fulfilment, we will need to identify what is right for us, what matters to us, what actually makes us happy and find the strength of will to follow through in attaining this, regardless of the opinions of others.

I do, however, add a proviso here.

Attaining what we personally aspire to should not be at the expense of others or damaging and disrespectful of someone else's unique differences!

Mindfulness Meets Emotional Awareness

The moment our actions involve maneuvering or manipulating others at their expense it is ultimately we ourselves who pay the price.

There is no self-respect in stepping on someone else to achieve one's own ends. Regardless of appearances and outward bravado, this simply fuels low self-esteem, an inner emptiness and a core sense of isolation.

A Useful Exercise.

Write a list of the kind of life that you would like to have. No holds barred, your hope and your dreams.

Canadian author Robin Sharma wrote that *"everything is created twice, first in the mind, then in reality."*

Allow your mind to wander and give yourself permission to dream.

Consider all the things that you would actually like, including the qualities of the person that you wish to nurture and support in yourself.

However, whilst doing this exercise also take some time to consider the reality of what it would be like to be in this position. What would a lifestyle like this really mean for you?

Now bring to mind someone who you see as a successful human being and find inspirational.

When I say successful, I am talking about contentment and personal happiness. What is it about them that makes you see them in this way? Use the following questions to help you to write a list.

- What it is about them as a human being that is so inspirational to you?
- What kind of attitudes do they have?
- What values do they have?
- What about them do you identify with?
- In terms of their material circumstances and physical achievements in the world, how did they arrive in this position?

If their circumstances have come about through sheer hard work and determination make a list of the qualities that they have that have enabled them to achieve this. Do they for example display a positive attitude, passion, motivation, an inner peacefulness, personal resilience?

Consider also what price they may also have had to pay to get to this position. For example, if they are an athlete, have they had to forgo their social life in order to maintain their training commitments?

If successful in business, have they had to work excessively long hours, maybe even on top of a day job, to eventually arrive at a position of success?

If they are a contented stay-at-home parent, perhaps they had to forgo some of their own career opportunities or lifestyle to remain at home?

Mindfulness Meets Emotional Awareness

If they have inherited wealth, they may have lived a childhood being ostracized for their position excluded from certain everyday activities that most of us would take for granted. They might also have experienced a falseness in people whose only desire to know them is due to their position in life, rather than for who they actually are as unique individual human beings.

Now write a list of the qualities of a human being that would make up the kind of person that you wish to be.

What kind of qualities, attitudes and values do you need to cultivate in yourself to embody and become your own hero?

- What matters to you and what are the most important things in your life?
- What are your values?
- How do these values contribute in making you the person that you are and in the development of your personal self-worth and self-esteem?
- How do you demonstrate these qualities in your daily life already and what areas of yourself are you proud of?

For example, if kindness is an important quality to you, how do you demonstrate this in your everyday world, to yourself as well as to others? If motivation is important to you, how do you demonstrate this in everyday ways? If validation and appreciation are important to you, how do you show these to both yourself and others?

People who really flourish do so because they feel good about themselves.

Mindfulness Meets Emotional Awareness

Regardless of their external achievements they fundamentally feel good about themselves. Their self-esteem feels good.

They live honorably and decently and regardless of the circumstances of their lives whatever they do they come away from the situation feeling good about themselves.

As a consequence, fulfilment comes naturally and when doorways of opportunity open, they are confident in grasping those opportunities. They can also evaluate their experiences in ways that finds personal growth in every situation and from every moment.

Now go about your daily life.

Hold the energy of your vision.

Do everything from a position of striving to be the very best that you can be. Whether you are hanging out the washing, cleaning up, making a sandwich, performing life-saving surgery or taking time to listen to someone — cultivate an attitude of being the best that you can be, right now!

Develop a pride in what you do and foster value in yourself and in others.

Each day take time to reflect and consider your day.

How have you felt?
When have you felt at your best?
If something didn't go so well, how have you gained from the experience and what have you learned?

Mindfulness Meets Emotional Awareness

Each day take time to celebrate your achievements, including the learning curve that comes from mindful non-critical evaluation.

Develop a mindset of possibility and give yourself permission to take opportunities as and when they present themselves to you.

"Infuse your life with action. Don't wait for it to happen. Make it happen. Make your own future. Make your own hope. Make your own love.
And whatever your beliefs, honour your creator, not by passively waiting for grace to come down from upon high, but by doing what you can to make grace happen...
yourself, right now, right down here on Earth."

Bradley Whitford (b. 1959), actor

Conclusion

Taking Responsibility and an "Ownership" of our Emotions.

"You must be the change you wish to see in the world."

Mahatma Gandhi (1869–1948), leader

When I was a little girl, I was given a bicycle for my birthday. I proudly took it to school, overjoyed with my gift. When I arrived at school gates one of the girls in my class met me there.

She took one look at my bicycle and she said:

"Is that all you got? When it was my birthday, I got a bicycle and a tape recorder and three records and £100 and a whole outfit with patent shoes and everything!"

By the time that she had finished with me, my bicycle seemed a minimal gift and something really rather unworthy, and my joy had in fact turned to envy. I felt inferior to her and envious of the fact that she had been given so much.

In truth and on reflection as an adult, I doubt that she had received any of those things.

Mindfulness Meets Emotional Awareness

In truth and on reflection as an emotionally aware adult, I suspect she was extremely envious of my bicycle and envious of my joy but unable to own her feelings, her reaction to me was one that in fact passed her envy over to me.

Emotions are a transferrable commodity.

She walked away feeling rather good about herself, and I walked away feeling less than good and envious of her. The very emotion that she had started with had been effectively passed over to me.

Envy is an emotion easily passed over to others in this way, as are fear, anger, disappointment, guilt… indeed, all of our most challenging emotions can be passed to others in this way, through both words and action. People can behave in a way that literally gives us something of their experience! They pass us their unwanted emotional package.

Likewise, emotions can be contagious, shared in a way that doesn't simply hand an emotional package over to someone else so that it is no longer felt as in my example above, but passed in a way that spreads and magnifies.

Now if this is an emotion such as happiness then the outcome is simply marvelous, we all feel good! Fantastic!

However, when we move into the realms of fear, anger, indeed any of our more potentially destructive emotions, when misused, these emotions can spread like an epidemic with individuals, communities and whole nations overwhelmed and swept along by the power of the collective tide losing sight of any capacity for reflective thought and personal choice.

Mindfulness Meets Emotional Awareness

We see this time and again in situations around us in the immediacy of our own lives as well as on a more global scale. The tragedy being that when powerful emotions are discharged without any awareness of personal responsibility not only do people get hurt but this kind of emotional reactivity inevitably generates more of the same.

Unaware of their emotions people spill over, lashing out at others creating drama and crises which in turn will inevitably fuel even more of the same powerful emotions.

If someone lashes out or behaves badly towards us it can be instinctive to react with retaliation thus generating a cycle that perpetuates and fuels the very same unmanageable emotions. When this happens on a larger scale, entire nations can be swept along in a frenzy of emotionally reactive behavior often with desperately destructive consequences.

We are living in a highly reactive world.

Just the other day I found myself considering the kinds of global problems that we as humanity are facing and I began to divide them into roughly two categories.

The first is that of natural disaster, the kinds of problems and challenges that we encounter in the face of drought, earthquakes, and other natural phenomena.

Mindfulness Meets Emotional Awareness

The second category, which far outweighed the first both in quantity as well as quality in terms of the challenges that we face in trying to find and establish some sort of resolvability, were the man-made problems. The kinds of problems that we as humanity face as a direct result of our own actions. Violence, war, hatred, prejudice, starvation when there is actually enough food to go around… the list goes on.

When we really break these difficulties down to their primary core drivers, almost all of our man-made problems could be resolved if we could only relate well with one another.

If we could learn to live in a manner that was mutually responsive and considerate of one another, with respectful negotiation being taught and indeed being lived, as a core foundational life skill.

If fascinates me that in the middle of a war zone, if a natural disaster occurs, for example an earthquake, on humanitarian grounds a ceasefire will be called and all parties will step up and help one another. In the face of an external problem mankind unites and joins together in mutual support. And not only do we support one another, but we enjoy it.

In the face of a crisis people love to help one another.

Now what this demonstrates to me is that at a core level of being, fundamentally we do enjoy being in relationship with each other in a way that is mutually supportive and beneficial to all. It feels good, not only to the recipients in need of help, but it also feels good for those who are giving as well!

Mindfulness Meets Emotional Awareness

However, when this external situation has been attended to and the immediate crisis is over, all parties will then go back to the primary position of war. They will return to fighting one another, with the direct intention to cause damage, potentially to the very people that the week before they were digging out of a pile of rubble in an attempt to save lives!

They have returned to a place of doing what they believe they 'have' to do! Doing what they perceive to be the only solution to some kind of difference between them.

At the very core of this there is an innate inability to resolve problems that sit between us. In the face of a natural disaster, in the face of a problem that is external to us, we demonstrate that we are not only capable of overriding our differences but that we also all benefit from doing so and yet when faced with a problem between us, we find a profound inability to negotiate in a way that is respectfully supportive of our differences and mutually beneficial to all.

As an emotionally orientated person this makes no sense to me, it doesn't 'feel' right. And even if I disengage from the way that I feel and I approach this from a place of purely logical thinking I can find no logic in this either!

It is curious that in my work with couples over many years I have seen exactly the same core problem replicated again and again. When either party is facing an external problem, they are monumentally supportive of one another and yet when either one has a problem with the other there is a complete inability to talk this through in a way that would demonstrate any form of mutual respect with a desire to consider each other's position and more importantly to consider and be responsive to one another's feelings.

It is as though emotions can only be heard and expressed when directed outwards at a common enemy rather than understand as a tool that fuels a mutuality of respectful and mindful giving and receiving. The kind of giving and receiving that enhances the quality and bond of a real relationship. One in which our imperfections and mistakes are valued as part of a learning curve and a way of growing together, rather than an area of vulnerability to be criticized and targeted and used as a weapon.

A breakdown in our ability to hear one another creates an arena between us of competition. We see this all around us, not only within intimate partnerships, but within our families and friendships, in our communities, in government and between nations.

Perhaps we are all so desperate to be heard that we have forgotten how to listen to one another.

It is my own view that to really take an ownership of self-responsibility in adulthood, we will need to be able to listen to ourselves.

How else can we possibly ever hope to live in a manner that is genuinely responsive and fully relational? If we are unable to listen to our own thoughts, feelings and opinions with value and appreciation, we are highly unlikely to be fully available to hear and receive the thoughts, feelings and opinions of others with an openness and receptivity that values our differences as an opportunity for learning and mutual growth.

Mindfulness Meets Emotional Awareness

As adults, in this we have a choice. We can each make a personal commitment to learn to listen to ourselves and in doing so develop our ability to communicate our feelings and needs to others.

As each of the chapters of this book have unfolded, I have found myself coming back time and again to the importance of healthy self-esteem.

Our belief that it's okay to express our feelings and our needs with an expectation of being heard is underpinned by our self-esteem. Our resilience and our emotional durability, indeed our capacity to look both within… and without, with kindness, compassion and a desire for enquiry, sits on a baseline of strong, solid, healthy self-esteem.

When we lack self-esteem, if our self-worth and self-value are fragile then engaging our mind in the process of calm, gentle, compassionate reflection can be a significant challenge.

The stronger our self-esteem, the greater our capacity to recognize our feelings as valid.

The stronger our self-esteem the greater our capacity to press that pause button, take time to listen to ourselves and to evaluate before taking a considered course of action.

The stronger our self-esteem, the greater our capacity to hold firm and regardless of external events, make choices that are congruent with our core inner values, the values that make us who we are and define us as unique individual human beings.

Mindfulness Meets Emotional Awareness

Whether we use our emotions to fuel actions of value or actions of destruction, will to a certain to extent be dependent upon our ability to engage with our emotions with an 'ownership' of the choices that they present us with in developing a life of self-responsibility with conscious action.

Central to living a more mindful life from a position of greater personal responsibility, is our ability to understand and engage with our emotions, not as an enemy and something to be feared, but as an ally, bringing us an emotionally enhanced experience of living that is taking us literally to 'the heart of the matter'. A life skill that enhances our capacity for healthy relational living.

The global implications caused by actions that are taken without thought or mindfulness of the consequences, or even worse actions that have been thought through with full awareness of the devastating consequences fueled by a desire to hurt and to cause damage, are heart breaking and can understandably leave us feeling as though the world is completely out of control! Certainly, out of our own control.

However, if we work on the premise that, even though we may not be fully aware of it, stemming from our own actions is a ripple effect that creates a wider impact in the world in general. Then in consciously developing a mindful connection with our emotions, a connection that supports our awareness of conscious, considered, reflected choice, on a daily basis, within the immediacy of our own world, each and every one of us has the capacity to create a more responsive, reflective humanity in which care and consideration form the basis of all of our relational exchanges.

Mindfulness Meets Emotional Awareness

Learning to listen and understand our emotions enables us to enhance our ability to use and to channel the extraordinary power and energy that emotions generate to good effect, not only for ourselves but for the world beyond us.

This choice is available to us, right here and right now.

My thought for today

"If we wish to see peace in the world, we will need to be peace in the world."

Mindfulness Meets Emotional Awareness

Review Request

If you have enjoyed this book and feel that it has been helpful to you then I would be very grateful if you would post a positive review. **Your support really does matter.**

Positive reviews encourage people to take a look inside and to potentially enhance their own journey of emotional discovery. Your reviews enable my message and my personal dedication to create positive change through personal empowerment to potentially reach a greater number of people.

To post a review all you have to do, is go to the review section of the books Amazon Page. There is a button that says: "Write a Customer Review". Click on this button and follow the prompts to post your review.

The links to the book on both Amazon.com and Amazon.co.uk are below. Thank you to those of you who have posted reviews on both.

Thank you beyond measure. I truly value your support and any feedback.
With much love and appreciation.

http://amzn.to/2x6bPLm Amazon.co.uk
http://amzn.to/2xEzFRs Amazon.com

Mindfulness Meets Emotional Awareness

About the Author and about this Series of Books.

"If our educational system taught our children to understand their feelings and to relate emotionally to themselves as well as to others, rather than focusing on and rewarding their ability to store information, the face of our world would change."

Jenny Florence.
Born 1961, Counsellor, Author & Writer, Speaker

Before committing fully to my career as a writer and speaker, I worked as an accredited counsellor for over 26 years. This has given me a good understanding of the kinds of difficulties that so many of us face within our daily lives and of course as a ordinary human being I have learned huge life lessons from my own life experiences.

As human beings, we are first and foremost relational beings, and yet curiously, it is within relationship and in the area of our relational skills where most of us seem to inevitably find our greatest and most frequent challenges.

Our emotions sit right at the heart of our relational exchanges. If we are to thrive and successfully navigate all that life throws at us, particularly in overcoming the kinds of difficulties that arise in our relationships and in the differences that sit between us, then developing our understanding of emotions and strengthening our capacity for emotional language and emotional communication will be a much needed core life skill.

In my own life, I have had some pretty challenging experiences including childhood depression, domestic violence in my adult life and the challenge of being a single Mum.

During the most difficult times in my life, whilst I clearly didn't enjoy the way that I was feeling, I can say without exception that every 'uncomfortable, uneasy' emotion that I felt was a natural response to a situation in my life that wasn't ok. These challenging emotions were giving me "good information" and I needed to learn listen to them, in order to find an appropriate and considered course of action.

Our emotions are a powerful, human commodity.
They can be our strongest and most supportive ally in life, or they can disable us, leaving us feeling blocked or at worst, out of control and in pieces.

In my experience, it is never the emotion itself that's the problem.

Our ability to listen to the information that our emotions bring and to then choose what we do with that information, from a position of mindful, considered thought will make the difference between a challenging life experience becoming a break through… or a break down.

I know that my deepening ability to listen to my emotions and to consider every emotional state that I feel as 'valuable information' has created a way of living that has, in itself, been completely life changing.

Mindfulness Meets Emotional Awareness

This is the second in my series of books about the intelligence of our emotions.

The format of this book is deliberate, with bite sized chapters designed to make it accessible, easy to read and above all translatable into a kind of emotional tool kit that can pragmatically help to integrate emotional awareness into daily living in ways that will enhance all aspects of who you are and who you wish to become.

Mindfulness Meets Emotional Awareness

Mindfulness Meets Emotional Awareness

Work with Jenny

Jenny is both a Writer and Speaker. She is also the Founder and Author of the A-Z of Emotional Health on-line Library, a Free Public Resource supporting all aspects of Mental and Emotional Health and Well-being.

Jenny can be contacted via her homepage of;
www.jennyflorencehealth.com

And via her on-line Library;
www.azemotionalhealth.com

References

Desmond Tutu.
https://www.brainyquote.com/quotes/quotes/d/desmondtut4
54152.html
Maria Shriver
https://www.brainyquote.com/quotes/quotes/m/mariashriv5
53677.html
John Gottman http://sourcesofinsight.com/emotional-
intelligence-quotes/
Fred Rogers http://www.goodreads.com/quotes/319182-part-
of-the-problem-with-the-word-disabilities-is-that
Daniel Goleman
https://www.goodreads.com/author/quotes/829.Daniel_Gole
man
Katherine Woodward Thomas
http://katherinewoodwardthomas.com/
Doc Childre and Deborah Rozman
http://www.wishafriend.com/quotes/qid/3799/
Bear Grylls
https://www.everywishes.com/quotes/quote/21179/983
Serenity Prayer
https://en.wikipedia.org/wiki/Serenity_Prayer
Anthon St Maarten
https://www.goodreads.com/author/quotes/6154621.Anthon_
St_Maarten
Marge Kennedy
https://www.brainyquote.com/quotes/quotes/m/margekenne
403991.html
Marshall B Rozenburg
https://www.goodreads.com/author/quotes/40541.Marshall_
B_Rosenberg
Source Unknown

http://www.angermanagementresource.com/healthy-anger.html

William Arthur Ward
https://www.brainyquote.com/quotes/quotes/w/williamart190448.html

Conan O'Brien
https://www.brainyquote.com/quotes/quotes/c/conanobri452011.html

Henry David Thoreau
https://www.brainyquote.com/quotes/quotes/h/henrydavid103847.html

Looby Macnamara Earth Pathways Wall Calendar 2017

H. Jackson Brown
https://www.brainyquote.com/quotes/quotes/h/hjacksonb629141.html

Ralph Blum The Book of Runes

Elisabeth Kubler-Ross
https://www.brainyquote.com/quotes/quotes/e/elisabethk553966.html

Jean Vanier http://www.goodreads.com/quotes/637252-envy-comes-from-people-s-ignorance-of-or-lack-of-belief

Marianne Williamson
https://en.wikiquote.org/wiki/Marianne_Williamson

Robin Sharma http://www.goodreads.com/quotes/648499-everything-is-created-twice-first-in-the-mind-and-then

Robin Sharma http://www.robinsharma.com/

Bradley Whitford.
https://www.brainyquote.com/quotes/quotes/b/bradleywhi410518.html

Mahatma Gandhi
https://www.brainyquote.com/quotes/quotes/m/mahatmagan109075.html

Made in United States
North Haven, CT
01 November 2022

26185169R10117